IMMODEST ACTS

STUDIES IN THE HISTORY OF SEXUALITY

Guido Ruggiero and Judith C. Brown, *General Editors*

GUIDO RUGGIERO

THE BOUNDARIES OF EROS

Sex Crime and Sexuality in Renaissance Venice

JUDITH C. BROWN

IMMODEST ACTS

The Life of a Lesbian Nun in Renaissance Italy

IMMODEST ACTS

The Life of a Lesbian Nun
in Renaissance Italy

JUDITH C. BROWN

OXFORD UNIVERSITY PRESS
New York   Oxford

Oxford University Press
Oxford New York Toronto
Delhi Bombay Calcutta Madras Karachi
Petaling Jaya Singapore Hong Kong Tokyo
Nairobi Dar es Salaam Cape Town
Melbourne Auckland

and associated companies in
Beruit Berlin Ibadan Nicosia

First published in 1986 by Oxford University Press, Inc.,
200 Madison Avenue, New York, New York 10016
First issued as an Oxford University Press paperback, 1986

Oxford is a registered trademark of Oxford University Press

Library of Congress Cataloging in Publication Data

Brown, Judith C.
Immodest acts.

1. Carlini, Benedetta. 2. Lesbian nuns—Italy—Biography.
3. Lesbianism—History. 4. Lesbians—Attitudes.
5. Women—Sexual behavior—History. I. Title.
BX4705.C3134B76 1986 306.7′663′0924 [B] 85-5031
ISBN 0-19-503675-1
ISBN 0-19-504225-5 (pbk.)

Printing (last digit): 9 8 7 6 5
Printed in the United States of America

TO SIMONA

Acknowledgments

When I first encountered the materials for this story, I thought I would be writing a footnote to another book. Many pages and many years later the footnote has become a book of its own. This transformation was possible because of the aid I received from many scholars and institutions along the way.

Financial support came from a fellowship given to me by the American Philosophical Society, which allowed me to supplement research in the State Archives of Florence and Pisa with an examination of materials at the Vatican Archives. I would like to thank the staff of all these institutions for their courteous help.

Other kinds of scholarly support and encouragement came from many individuals whose advice, criticism, and willingness to share unpublished manuscripts were of immense help. My scholarly debts are too numerous to cite in their entirety, but I would like to give special recognition to Judith Armstrong, Charmarie Blaisdell, Caroline Bynum, Sherrill Cohen, Estelle Freedman, Kent Gerard, Richard Goldthwaite, Stephen Greenblatt, Maryanne Horowitz, Victoria Kirkham, Ruth Liebowitz, Mary R. O'Neill, Elizabeth Perry, Richard Trexler, Guido Ruggiero, and Elissa Weaver. I would also like to thank my colleagues in modern European history at Stanford University, who read my initial forays into this project and gave useful suggestions for expanding various lines of inquiry. Needless to say, not all the readers of this book agreed with all of its contents. I am grateful, however, for the aid they extended and take responsibility for any errors of fact or interpretation that remain.

As is customary and appropriate for authors, I also wish to extend my thanks to my family. My children's acceptance of their mother's idiosyncrasies made it possible to engage in this project, and their well-justified lack of patience brought it to a timely end. My husband, as always, has been a loving supporter and critic from the earliest research to the final draft. His generosity of spirit and his sense of humor have been a constant source of strength. Finally, I would like to dedicate this book to my sister, Simona Miller, to whom I owe an intellectual and emotional debt that I will never be able to repay. Her independence and intellectual curiosity were models I held before me in my youth. She has been sister, mother, mentor, and friend. I hope that this offering will convey a small measure of my affection.

Stanford, California   J.C.B.
May 1985

Contents

IMMODEST ACTS

Introduction

I FOUND BENEDETTA CARLINI by chance, while leafing through an inventory of nearly forgotten documents in the State Archive of Florence. The entry in the inventory read: "Papers relating to a trial against Sister Benedetta Carlini of Vellano, abbess of the Theatine nuns of Pescia, who pretended to be a mystic, but who was discovered to be a woman of ill repute."[1] What prompted me to look at that book of entries is something I shall never know for certain. Perhaps it was the title that intrigued me more than anything else: *Miscellanea Medicea*—what odd and fascinating documents might be found there? The State Archive, I knew, was filled with some of the richest historical treasures in all of Europe and a collection of miscellaneous documents belonging to the Medici period was sure to contain interesting materials, especially for a historian about to embark on a study of the first Medici grand duke. My curiosity was piqued further because no one in the archive or in the books I consulted seemed to know who had gathered these particular documents into a collection or what purpose they might have had. I thought then that if I failed to look at what the *Miscellanea* contained, I would always wonder what I had missed.

The entry about Benedetta immediately caught my attention for several reasons. Her place of origin was of interest because I was finishing revisions on a manuscript about Renaissance Pescia. Any additional information on the town or its people could be incorporated into the text. But there was also something else that was striking about the entry. What had this nun done to merit such harsh words from the twentieth-century archivist who had read and inventoried the document?

My first conjecture was that she had probably had some sexual encounters with the priests who visited her convent. Such affairs were commonplace in the Renaissance. Convents were notorious for their loose moral standards and for their sexual license, which is not surprising because they were less often the homes of women with a strong religious vocation than warehouses for the discarded women of middle-class and patrician families.

Instead of such affairs, however, what I found was something quite different and totally unexpected. The document, roughly one hundred unnumbered pages, consisted of a series of ecclesiastical investigations that took place from 1619 to 1623 into the visions and miraculous claims of Benedetta Carlini, Abbess of the Convent of the Mother of God. The investigations contained, among other things, a detailed description of her sexual relations with another nun. This makes the document unique for premodern Europe and invaluable for analyzing hitherto unexplored areas of women's sexual lives as well as Renaissance views of female sexuality.

Had the material belonged to a later epoch, the sexual allegations against Benedetta would not have been all that rare. Indeed, in Protestant countries and in those intellectual circles in Catholic countries that placed themselves in opposition to the Church, the love of nuns for one another became a literary topos—yet one more nasty charge against a corrupt institution.[2] But such accusations of homosexual relations behind convent walls were meant to elicit a smirk. Like many such slanders, they may have contained a grain of truth, but even in the eighteenth century they were unsubstantiated.

I wondered, therefore, as I read about Benedetta whether the account of her life written by the ecclesiastical officials might not be equally spurious. Having come to their attention through the extraordinary mystical claims she made and the popular following she was beginning to acquire, Benedetta may have posed a threat to the authority of the church. False charges about her sexual purity might silence her more effectively than simple attempts to discredit her claims to divine favors. In pre-modern Europe, women were thought to be much more lustful than men and easily given to debauchery. Vast quantities of literature—medical, legal, and theological—going back to Aristotle and the Bible had demonstrated the point to the satisfaction of contemporary opinion.[3] As a result, accusations against women on the grounds of sexual misconduct were rather frequent. Women accused of witchcraft, for instance, were often said to have been seduced by the devil because they enjoyed sexual intercourse with him. So pervasive was this notion that even some of the victims of these charges voluntarily came forth with detailed accounts of what it was like to make love to the devil.[4]

But if such instances made me ponder the authenticity of the charges against Benedetta, the fact that in almost all cases the object of women's sexual desires were said to be men lends credence to the veracity of the allegations against her. If the authorities had sought merely to taint her reputation for chastity, it would have been simpler for them both, from a circumstancial as well as an intellectual point of view, to elaborate a story of sexual misconduct involving a particular priest with whom Benedetta had occasionally been seen in compromising situations.

For Europeans had long found it difficult to accept that women could actually be attracted to other women. Their view of human sexuality was phallocentric—women might be attracted to men and men might be attracted to men but there was nothing in a woman that could long sustain the sexual desires of another woman. In law, in medicine, and in the public mind, sexual relations between women were therefore ignored. Among the hundreds if not thousands of cases of homosexuality tried by lay and ecclesiastical courts in medieval and early modern Europe, there are almost none involving sexual relations between women. References to a few prosecutions have turned up in Spain. There are four sketchily known cases in France, two in Germany, one in Switzerland, one in the Netherlands, and none, until now, in Italy.[5]

This obliteration of a significant aspect of female sexuality from contemporary consciousness is all the more curious because at some level of knowledge, people were well aware that it existed. In his epistle to the Romans, St. Paul, referring to pagans who rejected the one true God, had stated: "God gave them up unto vile affections: for even their women did change the natural use into that which is against nature" (Romans 1:26). Exactly what Paul had in mind is not clear, but from the earliest days of the church, his words were interpreted by many as a reference to sexual relations between women. Explaining this passage in the fourth century, St. Ambrose (d. 397) stated: "He testifies that, God being angry with the human race because of their idolatry, it came about that a woman would desire a woman for the use of foul lust."[6] To which St. John Chrysostom (d. 407) added that "it is even more shameful that the women should seek this type of intercourse, since they ought to have more modesty than men."[7]

Similar interpretations were still to be found several hundred years later. St. Anselm's twelfth-century commentary on Romans 1:26 was: "Thus women changed their natural use into that which is against nature, because the women themselves committed shameful deeds with women."[8] And his younger contemporary, Peter Abelard, making sure the meaning was perfectly clear, glossed further, "Against nature, that is, against the order of nature, which created women's genitals for the use of men, and conversely, and not so women could cohabit with women."[9]

Because sexual relations between women offended the laws of God and nature, a number of early medieval manuals of penance include them in the catalogue of sins that clergy might find among their parishioners. In the seventh century, Theodore of Tarsus told clergy what to do "if a woman practices vice with a woman." The Venerable Bede also mentions sexual relations between women, as does Pope Gregory III in his eighth-century penitential.[10]

But without doubt the most widely influential book to guide Christian thought on the subject was St. Thomas Aquinas' *Summa theologiae*, which under the rubric of lust, subsumed four categories of vice against nature: masturbation, bestiality, coitus in an unnatural position, and "copulation with an undue sex, male with male and female with female."[11] Later theologians took their cue from St. Thomas, often citing him in their own work, as did, for example, Sylvester Prierias in his confessional manual and Jean Gerson, the fifteenth-century rector of the University of Paris, who included sex between women, along with "semination in a vessel not ordained for it," in his list of crimes against nature.[12] Similarly, the Archbishop of Florence, St. Antoninus (1363–1451), included lesbian sexuality as the eighth of nine categories of lustful sins, although in a rather odd twist for a writer of his time, he differentiated it from sins against nature, which were comprised of lustful acts between a man and a woman "outside of the natural place where children are made." Finally, St. Charles Borromeo's penitential, written in the late sixteenth century, included sex between women: "If a woman fornicates by herself or with another woman she will do two years' penance."[13]

Awareness of lesbian sexuality among a few ecclesiastical leaders led to some efforts to curb it in monastic communities. As early as 423, St. Augustine had warned his sister, who had taken holy vows, that "The love which you bear one another ought not to be carnal, but spiritual: for those things which are practiced by immodest women, even with other females, in shameful jesting and playing, ought not to be done even by married women or by girls who are about to marry, much less by widows or chaste virgins dedicated by a holy vow to be handmaidens of Christ."[14] To remove temptation, the councils of Paris (1212) and Rouen (1214) prohibited nuns from sleeping together and required a lamp to burn all night in dormitories. From the thirteenth century on, monastic rules usually called for nuns to stay out of each others' cells, to leave their doors unlocked so that the abbess might check on them, and to avoid special ties of friendship within the convent. The reasons for the rules were, of course, always implicit. No details were given of what practices the nuns might fall into if their cells were locked, although it is obvious from the evidence of a surviving poem sent by one nun to another, that the subjects of the legislation did not lack imagination.[15]

In the secular world there were also occasional references to lesbian sexuality. A few jurists concerned with civil law, for example, discussed the issue. In the early fourteenth century, Cino da Pistoia erroneously believed that the *lex foedissimam*, a Roman imperial edict of 287 A.D., referred to relations between women. "This law," which actually was meant to protect the rights of rape victims, according to Cino, "can be understood in two ways: first, when a woman suffers defilement by surrendering to a male; the other way is when a woman suffers defilement in surrendering to another woman. For there are certain women, inclined to foul wickedness, who exercise their lust on other women and pursue them like men." This interpretation was followed by Bartholomaeus de Saliceto (1400), whose glosses were widely used in the next few centuries.[16] Yet despite these writings, there appears to be little civil legislation that took up the issue. Among the scant mentions of lesbian sexuality in secular laws are a provision in the Constitution of the Holy Roman Empire, promulgated by Charles V in 1532, and a statute adopted in Treviso in 1574. Most civil laws against same sex relations, including the English act of 1533, which made buggery punishable by death, did not specifically mention women. Yet they were quite explicit about the acts committed by males and the penalties that should be imposed on them.[17]

In light of the knowledge that Europeans had about the possibility of lesbian sexuality, their neglect of the subject in law, theology, and literature suggests an almost active willingness to *dis*believe. A characteristic remark is that attributed to Anastasius with reference to Romans 1:26— "Clearly [the women] do not mount each other but, rather, offer themselves to the men."[18] Compared to the frequency with which male homosexuality is mentioned, especially after the thirteenth century, in canon and civil law, in penitentials and confessional manuals, and in popular sermons and literature, the handful of documents citing the love of women for one another is truly scant.[19] In a period of roughly fifteen hundred years, they amount to no more than a dozen or so scattered references. Even Peter Damian's *Book of Gomorrah* (ca. 1051), a long and detailed diatribe against homosexual acts, confines itself to the misdeeds of men.[20] One looks in vain for the hellfire, and brimstone condemnations of the sort that popular preachers hurled against what they called "the clerical vice."[21] And a search of secular literature for the kinds of homosexual relations commonly attributed to men yields virtually nothing about women until mid-seventeenth century. Dante, whose harrowing journey takes him past all the known varieties of human sins, does not include female sodomites either in Hell or Purgatory. Indeed, the male gender of the sodomites is implicit in the remarks he attributes to Brunetto Latino: "We all were clerks and men of youth, great men of letters, scholars of renown; all by the one same crime defiled on earth."[22]

Similarly, Boccaccio, who was not averse to exposing the sexual misdeeds of men and women, did not even hint that this variety of sexual conduct existed. And Ariosto, who comes closest to depicting erotic feelings between women, ultimately dismisses the possibility. In his *Orlando Furioso*, Fiordispina's love for Bradamanete goes unfulfilled when the latter reveals that she is a woman. After bewailing her fate, which she believes is unprecedented in the annals of history, Fiordispina remains chaste, despite sleeping in a bed shared with Bradamante. Her difficulties are not solved until Ricciardeto, Bradamante's twin brother, appears on the scene and consummates the relationship.[23]

Why sexual relations between women were either ignored or dismissed in this way is amply clear from the few authors who did write about them. In his *Ragionamenti amorosi*, the sixteenth-century Italian writer, Agnolo Firenzuola, sets his female characters to debating why it would not be better for a woman to love another woman since she would thus avoid any risk to her chastity. After a lengthy argument, he comes to the conclusion that this kind of love would not be preferable because the beauty of men, by a decree of nature, inspires greater desire in a woman than does the beauty of other women. The same kind of attraction to the opposite sex holds true for men. As proof, he observed that no man can see a beautiful woman without feeling a natural desire to please her and so it is with a woman at the sight of a beautiful man.[24]

More eager to admit the existence of erotic attractions between women, Brantôme, the late-sixteenth century commentator on the sexual antics of French courtiers, observed that lately, after "the fashion was brought from Italy by a lady of quality who I will not name," sexual relations between women have become very common. Some of these were young girls and widows who preferred to make love to each other than "to go to a man and thus become pregnant and lose their honor or their virginity. . . ."[25] Others were women who used other women to enhance their lovemaking with men: "Because this little exercise, as I have heard say, is nothing but an apprenticeship to come to the greater [love] of men; because after they are heated up and well on their way with one another, their heat does not diminish unless they bathe in a livelier and more active current. . . . Because in the end, as I have heard many ladies tell, there is nothing like a man; and what they get from other women is nothing but enticements to go and satisfy themselves with men."[26]

In short, whether common or rare, sexual relations between women could have only one purpose, to enhance and glorify real sex, i.e., sex with a man. This is one of the reasons why some contemporaries may have felt they could safely ignore lesbian sexuality. "Let us excuse the young girls and widows," wrote Brantôme, "for loving these frivolous and vain pleasures."[27] For him, as for many other men of his time, the attraction of women for each other was not to be taken seriously.

Another reason for ignoring lesbian sexuality was the belief that women, who were thought to be naturally inferior to men, were merely trying to emulate them: "it is better that a woman give herself over to a libidinous desire to do as a man, than that a man make himself effeminate; which makes him out to be less courageous and noble. The woman, accordingly, who thus imitates a man, can have a reputation for being more valiant and courageous than another."[28] While such reasoning did not condone sex between women, it placed it within a long Western tradition in which women, like all other creatures, tried to ascend to a more perfect state of nature. Paradoxically, such relations tended to reaffirm, rather than subvert, the assumed biological hierarchy, in which "the body of a man is as superior to that of a woman as the soul is to the body."[29]

These notions were supported further by the observations and writings of physicians. Some had noted that in a few cases women did not just imitate men, but actually became men. These sex changes wrought by nature always worked in one direction, from female to male. There were no recorded instances of reverse transformations. Perfection was not likely to degenerate into imperfection.

The findings of physicians and antomists with regard to female reproductive organs also influenced views of lesbian sexuality in another way. Although it was commonly believed that women had testes (what later came to be called ovaries), which produced semen, their semen was thought to be colder, less active, and in most respects less important in human reproduction than that of men. The notion that they could pollute each other like men through the spilling of seed in the wrong vessel was therefore generally dismissed. In a society that had such imperfect knowledge of human biology and that in the process of procreation valued the male sperm above all else, the waste of male seed was thought a worse offense against the laws of God and nature than was the misuse of the seed or reproductive organs of women.[30]

Thus, for a number of reasons, most of the writers concerned with establishing penalties for lesbian acts tended to be more lenient toward them than toward male homosexuality. Theodore of Tarsus, for example, prescribed a penance of three years for any woman who "practices vice with a woman," the same as if "she practices solitary vice." In contrast, "fornication" between males was to be atoned through a penance of ten years.[31] The penintential of Gregory III prescribed 160 days for women who engaged in sex with other women and one year or more for male homosexuality.[32] And Charles Borromeo's penitential meted out two years' penance if a woman "fornicated" with another woman or by herself while giving men seven to fifteen years of penance, depending on their marital status, for engaging in coitus with another man.[33]

Yet, the tendency to view lesbian sexuality as a lesser offense was not unanimous. Some authorities viewed it on a par with male homosexuality and therefore punishable by death. What appears to be the earliest secular law to mention sexual relations between women, a statute in a late thirteenth-century French law code, states: "Those men who have been proved to be sodomites must lose their c___ [?] And if anyone commits this offense a second time, he must lose a member. And if he does it a third time, he must be burned. A woman who does this shall lose a member each time, and on the third must be burned."[34] Bartholomaeus de Saliceto, in the fifteenth century, also recommended the death penalty.[35] But it was not until the sixteenth century, when the Catholic and Protestant reformations brought about a growing concern with legislating moral conduct, as well as curbing heresy, an offense traditionally associated with homosexuality,[36] that such harsh views became common in the few laws and juridical commentaries that discussed the subject.[37] The two laws of the period that specifically mentioned women in connection with same-gender sex both provided the death sentence. Charles V's statute of 1532 states: "if anyone commits impurity with a beast, or a man with a man, or a woman with a woman, they have forfeited their lives and shall, after the common custom, be sentenced to death by burning."[38] Treviso's law similarly noted that

"If . . . a woman commits this vice or sin against nature, she shall be fastened naked to a stake in the Street of Locusts and shall remain there all day and night under a reliable guard, and the following day shall be burned outside the city."[39] In Spain, Gregorio Lopez' mid-sixteenth century gloss on the country's basic law code, *Las Siete Partidas* (1256), reflected this hardening stance by extending the death penalty to women. Although the original code had not mentioned them, Lopez observed that "Women sinning in this way are punished by burning according to the law of their Catholic Majesties which orders that this crime against nature be punished with such a penalty, especially since the said law is not restricted to men, but refers to any person of whatever condition who has unnatural intercourse."[40]

Even among those who believed in the death penalty for such acts, however, there were further disagreements. Whereas Lopez thought that the death penalty applied in all cases, his compatriot, Antonio Gomez (b. 1501), felt that burning should be mandatory only in cases in which "a woman has relations with another woman by means of any material instrument." If, on the other hand, "a woman has relations with any woman without an instrument," then a lighter penalty such as beating could be applied.[41] The distinctions were carried one step further by the Italian jurist Prospero Farinacci (1554–1618). Taken at its most general, if a woman "behaves like a man with another woman," according to Farinacci, "she will be in danger of the penalties for sodomy and death." But looking at the particulars, if a woman simply made overtures to another woman, she should only be denounced publicly. "If she behaves corruptly with another woman only by rubbing," she is to be subject to an unspecified "punishment," and "if she introduces some wooden or glass instrument into the belly of another," she should be put to death.[42]

What lies behind these disagreements about how to deal with lesbian sexuality is more than just a difference in time and place, especially since most of the writers were working out of the same tradition of Roman and canon law. Furthermore, by the sixteenth century, many of their writings were printed and widely circulated throughout Europe. Their discussions of the issue, whether in medical, legal, or other types of literature betray a fundamental ignorance about what women did with each other and how that fit into established sexual categories and sexual crimes. In his work on *The Good of Marriage*, for example, St. Augustine, whose thoughts on sex were fundamental to shaping the Western tradition, defined as "unnatural and sinful those sexual acts in which intercourse did not take place in a vessel fit for procreation."[43] In theory this rubric is so broad that it could include everything from coitus interruptus to lesbian sexuality. But the specific practices decried by Augustine in this essay were male homosexuality and anal intercourse among heterosexual couples, which he considered even worse. Since a woman possessed a natural organ that a man might use for copulation, not to do so required a more active willingness to sin. Augustine's only allusion to lesbian sexuality comes up in another context, as one of many subjects on which he advises his sister, who is trying to govern a monastic community. He obviously attaches no particular weight to it.[44]

In the seventh century, Theodore of Tarsus placed the vice that one woman practices with another alongside solitary vice in meting out penances for women. By way of contrast, he split his discussion of "fornication" between males from that of male masturbation, and also prescribed quite different penalties for the two sins.[45]

Two generations later Gregory III separated sodomy from the category of "minor sins" that included "coitus between women," masturbation (probably referring to

mutual masturbation), and heterosexual anal intercourse.[46] In the thirteenth century, however, Albertus
Magnus linked both male and female homosexuality to
new and emerging notions about nature. The result was
that lesbian, like male homosexual, acts were now labeled
sodomy: "a sin against nature, male with male and female
with female."[47] Albertus' pupil, St. Thomas Aquinas,
adopted the same view. As with other forms of lust, sodomy, according to Aquinas, was a sin by which human
beings lost their reason while engaged in venereal acts.
But it formed part of a subspecies of lust—sins against
nature—in which the sexual act was directed solely at
pleasure and did not permit procreation. Such acts included, from the least sinful to the most, masturbation,
heterosexual intercourse in unnatural positions, sodomy,
and bestiality. All of these differed from other forms of
lust, such as rape, adultery, and the like, which did not
subvert the natural order of God's creation.[48]

  In this, as in so many other aspects of moral theology,
the Thomistic view held sway for the next few centuries.
Yet the ambiguities continued, perhaps because Aquinas
did not specify sexual acts to the precise degree that some
later writers did, and perhaps also because even those
moralists who cited him did not always understand fully
what Aquinas had written. Thus in addition to sodomy,
St. Antoninus (d. 1459) listed eight other forms of lust:
fornication, deflowering (*stupro*), rape, adultery, incest,
sacrilege (intercourse with a cleric or nun), masturbation,
and lust against nature. Sodomy, in this scheme was "lust,
male with male and female with female;" while lust against
nature occurred "when a male lusts with a female outside
of the natural place where children are made."[49] Charles
Borromeo (d. 1584), who accepted the Thomistic definition
of sodomy as coitus against nature, on the other hand,
imagined it only as a male vice.[50] The acts of women came
under the category of fornication, a sin of lust that was

not unnatural, and which included adultery and rape. Vincent Fillucio, who followed Aquinas in distinguishing between masturbation (*mollitia*) and sodomy (*sodomia*) in both men and women, added that in order to have true sodomy there had to be "consummated carnal copulation," by which he meant ejaculation.[51] This distinction was also adopted by Dominicus Raynaldus, for whom simple penetration with no ejaculation constituted *stuprum*, which was punishable by death, but not by death followed by burning.[52] Implicit in his discussion is the view that sodomy was basically anal intercourse. And indeed, according to one writer, in ordinary speech, as distinct from the writings of learned men, by the seventeenth century, sodomy had come to mean just that.[53]

The conceptual difficulties contemporaries had with lesbian sexuality is reflected in the lack of an adequate terminology. *Lesbian* sexuality did not exist. Neither, for that matter, did *lesbians*. Although the word "lesbian" appears once in the sixteenth century in the work of Brantôme, it was not commonly used until the nineteenth, and even then was applied first to certain acts rather than a category of persons.[54] Lacking a precise vocabulary and precise concepts, a large array of words and circumlocutions came to be used to describe what women allegedly did: mututal masturbation, pollution, fornication, sodomy, buggery, mutual corruption, coitus, copulation, mutual vice, the defilment or impurity of women by one another. And those who did these terrible things, if called anything at all, were called fricatrices, that is women who rubbed each other, or Tribades, the Greek equivalent for the same action.[55]

The confusion on all these issues was so great and the veil of ignorance that hung over the sexual lives of women was so dense that in the late seventeenth century, a learned Italian cleric, Lodovico Maria Sinistrari, in an effort to clarify the issues, was moved to write extensively on what

he called female sodomy. "All moralists discuss this ig-
noble vice between women and teach that a veritable
Sodomy is committed between women." But, he laments,
"in what way no one explains."[56] This deplorable situation, he felt, was in immediate need of rectification, because in order to absolve the stray females in their flocks,
clerics had to know precisely what sins they had committed: "in practice, it is necessary for Confessors to be
able to discern the case in which women by touching each
other provoke themselves to voluntary pollution (*molli-
tiem*) and when they fall into the Sodomitical crime, in
order to come to a judgment about the gravity of the sin."
Another important reason for knowing was that in many
Catholic areas, sodomy was a serious enough sin that
judgments about penance and absolution were reserved
to bishops. After consulting many theological, legal, and
medical sources, Sinistrari defined sodomy as carnal intercourse in the wrong vessel. This includes heterosexual
anal intercourse and coitus between women, but excludes
mutual masturbation with any other part of the body or
the use of "material instruments." If there is insertion of
a finger or of an inanimate object, "there is neither coitus
nor copulation," and "there can in no way be Sodomy,
because Sodomy necessarily requires coitus. Instead there
is simple pollution, affected nevertheless by an aggravating quality, which does not change in the least the species
of the offense." The question, however, is "how can one
woman lie with another in such a way that their rubbing
against each other can be called Sodomy?" For Sinistrari,
"this is the heart of the problem." To solve it, he consulted
many of the latest medical treatises, including Thomas
Bartolin's *Anatomical Tables*, and came to the conclusion
that only those women who had an excessively large clitoris could engage in sodomy with each other. Likely
candidates to have this unfortunate condition were girls
who masturbated as children and women who had an

overabundance of heat and semen. But unlike Middle Eastern women, whose passions had to be curbed by surgical means, Western European women seldom found themselves in this predicament.[57]

This, of course, did not mean that female sodomy should be ignored. If charges were brought against a woman, she should be examined by competent midwives to determine if she was physiologically capable of committing the act. An enlarged clitoris was a presumption of guilt, which brought in its wake a sentence of death by hanging followed by burning at the stake. This was the punishment to be given to all sodomites, male or female: "the penalties mentioned above should be inflicted without exception."[58]

Harsh punishment was necessary both to avoid the wrath of God, who might otherwise destroy the world as he had Sodom and Gomorrah, and also for its deterrent effect. Sinistrari's recommendations to confessors for eliciting information from someone suspected of lesbian crimes point to the ancient fear that women, with their abundant capacity for lust and their limited capacity for reason, might start getting ideas if they heard of such goings-on. If a confessor had reason to suspect one of his parishioners, he should proceed with his questions "modestly and prudently." He should start at the most general level and gradually, depending on the answers received, get down to the specifics of the acts committed.[59]

Even more than male sodomy, sodomy between females was "the sin which cannot be named." In the fifteenth century, the confessional manual attributed to Jean Gerson called it a sin against nature in which "women have each other by detestable and horrible means which should not be named or written." In the next century, Gregorio Lopez referred to it as "the silent sin," *peccatum mutum*.[60] For this reason Germain Colladon, the famous sixteenth-century jurist, advised the Genevan authorities, who had no prior experience with lesbian crimes, that the death sentence should be read publicly, as it normally was in cases of male homosexuality, but that the customary description of the crime committed should be left out. "A crime so horrible and against nature," he wrote, "is so detestable and because of the horror of it, it cannot be named."[61] The problem was not just that Colladon had a particular abhorrence for this kind of offense, but that women, because of their weaker natures, were feared to be more susceptible to suggestion. Consequently, while men found guilty of sodomy were to have their crimes read aloud in order to deter others, sexual relations between women were better left unmentioned.

Crimes that could not be named, thus, literally had no name and left few traces in the historical record. The contradictory notions that Western Europeans had about women's sexuality made it impossible to discuss lesbian sexuality openly, if at all. Silence bred confusion and confusion bred fear. On these foundations Western society built an impenetrable barrier that has lasted for nearly two thousand years.[62]

This is why the ecclesistical investigation into the life of Benedetta Carlini, abbess of the Convent of the Mother of God, is so important. Here is one of the rare instances in which we can glimpse in actual practice and in considerable detail Western attitudes toward lesbian sexuality. In the process, we can also recreate and hold up to examination the social world in which these attitudes flourished. Benedetta Carlini was condemned by many of her contemporaries as well as by posterity. Yet condemnation of her behavior was not, and perhaps will not be, universal. In life she was an impressive and controversial figure and in death her story compels the attention that official pronouncements about her sought to deny. This then is the story of Benedetta Carlini, whose sins and whose life we may understand and not judge.

CHAPTER ONE

The Family

BENEDETTA'S STORY BEGINS in sixteenth-century Vellano, a remote mountain village perched on the slopes of the Appennines some forty-five miles northwest of Florence. The town, now as then, seems to defy the passage of time—crooked, narrow streets wind their way through the steep hillside, high medieval walls overlook silvery leaved olive trees and dense chestnuts; terraced fields carved from the meager earth surround the jumble of buildings; and beyond the cramped confines of the village and its fields, off in the distance, past the gradually descending hills, are the vast spaces of the Arno river valley barely visible on the horizon.

In this idyllic place, on the night of St. Sebastian of the year 1590, Benedetta Carlini was born. Her birth and childhood, as she recalled them years later, have a fairy-tale quality about them, with supernatural events and portents of significant things to come. Her birth was difficult. Her mother, Midea, had such a painful labor that the midwife who attended her came out to the room where her husband Giuliano was waiting to tell him that both mother and child might die shortly. When he heard this, Giuliano beseeched God on his knees to spare their lives. Soon thereafter, the midwife returned to tell him that his wife had given birth to a girl and that mother and daughter were well. In gratitude for God's intervention, Giuliano named the girl Benedetta—blessed—and he dedicated her to His service. Thus from the moment of her birth, Benedetta was destined to become a nun.

Accustomed as we are to the notion of self-determination, it may be difficult for us to understand and accept Giuliano's decision about his daughter's future—a decision made in total disregard for what her wishes might be once she grew up. Benedetta, however, was not alone in being denied a say in what to do with her own life. Most girls of her day were not consulted about the major decision of their lives, whether to enter a convent or marriage. That judgment was made by parents when their daughters were too young either to assent or object. To be sure, there were nuns who had strong religious vocation, and some even who entered the convent against the desires of their parents. Forced marriages and women's restricted place in the domestic setting made the life of the convent an attractive alternative for many. Moreover, in mid-sixteenth century the Council of Trent had reaffirmed as part of its church reform program the age-old position of the church that women were not to be coerced into becoming nuns but were to do so only of their own free will.[1] The sixteenth century, however, had different notions of what constituted coercion than does the twentieth; we cannot help wondering how much free will a young girl had when she was confronted by her parents and kinsmen and when, as was usually the case, the world of the convent was the only world she knew well. For most girls were brought there at a tender age, long before they had to take any vows. Their familiarity with the religious life and their fears of the alien world outside, not to say anything of threats of disinheritance, all would have worn down any overt resistance long be-

fore. Nothing is more revealing of many a girl's predicament than the diary notations made by a nun in the
convent Benedetta would join. One of these recorded the
arrival of Maria Maddalena di Giuliano Ceci, who "does
not want to be a nun." Several years later, routine entries
about other matters mention again the presence of Sister
Maria Maddalena among the nuns of the convent.[2] Arcangela Tarabotti, an early seventeenth-century Venetian
nun, called this kind of life a "monastic inferno" to which
the nuns were condemned by the tyranny of their fathers.[3]

The convent years, however, were still far away for
Benedetta, and if Giuliano was a "tyrant" he appears to
have been a benevolent one. Benedetta's recollection of
her family life suggests a loving environment in which
both parents "received much happiness" from their
daughter. Family life was also relatively secure from a
material point of view. Giuliano Carlini was the third
richest man among Vellano's eight hundred inhabitants.
In addition to his house in Vellano and several properties
scattered in the area, he owned a farm just outside of
town, where he and his family retired shortly after Benedetta's birth.[4] Possessions of this sort did not come to
everyone. And the Carlini did not think of themselves as
just anyone. Giuliano's wife, Midea d'Antonio Pieri, was
the sister of the parish priest, a pillar of the community
in any small European town of the early modern period.[5]
The Carlini were proud of their social standing, so much
so that they built a family tomb, something to remind the
living of the importance of the family and its place in the
community.

How Giuliano came by his possessions or how he added
to them is not clear. In the late sixteenth century, the
people of Vellano made their living by working the land
and raising a few sheep and other farm animals. The
Carlini most likely were no exception in owing their income to the land. Grain, olive oil, wine, and chestnut

flour—the staples of mountain people's diets in that region—loom large in Giuliano's will. But it is also probable that he did not work his land himself but hired a peasant or two to do it for him. The steep hillsides had to be worked by hand with a hoe because there was little room in them for plough animals. The stones were picked from the earth one by one and piled on one another to make the retaining walls that kept the mountain from sliding into the work of man. It was backbreaking labor that a literate man like Giuliano was not likely to do. His literacy qualified him for other occupations closed to most others in this remote rural world. He may have been a notary, or a doctor, or a small trader. The records are silent on the matter and we can only conjecture about the possibilities.

Much more can be known about Giuliano's domestic activities. For a Tuscan father, he was unusually involved in raising his daughter. Indeed, he virtually overshadowed his wife in all but the most routine or biologically linked activities having to do with her. Perhaps this was because she was an only child. Perhaps also Giuliano was more attentive to the lives of his female relations because he appears to have had no close male relatives. The records only mention his mother, his sister, his wife, and his daughter.[6] Whatever the reasons, Giuliano took charge of Benedetta's life in ways that left no doubt about his interest in her.

Immediately upon dedicating Benedetta to the religious life, he "went to tell her mother and she assented." He also "had her nursed and fed by her own mother," a rather unusual step for a man of his standing, who could afford to hire a wet-nurse. His insistence that Midea nurse her own child may have been prompted by the knowledge that babies did not survive as well in the hands of wet-nurses as in those of their mothers. Most wet-nurses were poor country women, too ill fed and ill clothed themselves to take adequate care of their overly numerous charges. He may also have been concerned that the moral character of the nurse would be transmitted to the child. It was commonly thought that both virtues and vices could be passed on through the mother's milk. In advising parents on the selection of wet-nurses, Renaissance moralists like Paolo da Certaldo counseled: "she should be prudent, well-mannered, honest, not a drinker or a drunkard, because very often children draw from and resemble the nature of the milk they suck."[7]

Given his concern for the welfare of his baby, it would not be surprising if Giuliano did not also abstain from sexual relations with his wife for about one and one half years after Benedetta's birth. Medical opinion held that a mother's milk became spoiled by sexual intercourse and pregnancy. It was precisely this requirement for sexual abstinence which, when added to the other demands made by a newborn on its mother, led so many middle- and upper-class Tuscan fathers to search for surrogate mothers for their infants. According to San Bernardino of Siena, "to procure themselves more pleasure," parents sent their offspring to an uncertain future at the hands of "a dirty drab."[8] Benedetta was spared such a fate.

Once she was old enough to receive an education, it was again Giuliano who provided it. Most Renaissance treatises on education suggest a clear division of labor. Small children of either sex were to receive their first lessons from their mothers. Past this stage, boys were to be educated in grammar schools by male teachers and girls were to continue their instruction at the hands of their mothers. Benedetta's education did not follow the norm.[9]

Her father was a devout man. He was particularly attached to a crucifix that he had in his home and he provided in his will that after his own and his wife's death his house should be turned into an oratory dedicated to the Mother of God.[10] Benedetta's education therefore was primarily a religious education. "At the age of five she knew the litany of the saints and other prayers which her father had taught her." Several times a day, under his tutelage she would take the Rosary and recite the litany. At the age of six she learned to read and to study the rudiments of Christian doctrine. She may even have learned a smattering of Latin.[11]

Benedetta's mother played some part in her upbringing but she was clearly very diffident about her function. She did instruct Benedetta to recite five Pater Nosters and eight Ave Marias every day, but on the whole she seems to have perceived her role as that of directing her daughter toward more powerful, supernatural female guides who could offer better protection than herself. She was especially devoted to St. Catherine of Siena, whose mystical marriage with Christ was celebrated as a feast day in Benedetta's home. She was also devoted to a statue of the Virgin that she acquired especially for Benedetta. Indeed, her devotion to the Virgin was so strong and her confidence in her own role as mother so limited that she "told Benedetta to take the Madonna as her mother and custodian."

What was it that Benedetta needed protection from? As in many folk tales, the protagonist of the story was early on confronted by destructive forces battling for her life and soul. One day a black dog appeared wanting to drag her away. The child's screams frightened him off, and by the time her mother came to her side, the dog had disappeared. Benedetta and her parents viewed this incident as the work of a supernatural agent. The devil had disguised himself as an animal in order to harm her. Henceforth she would have to take care.

Luckily, she did not have to face the danger alone. In addition to her parents, supernatural help came her way. One beautiful spring day, when Benedetta was standing on a small porch of her house singing her Lauds to the Virgin, she suddenly heard a nightingale imitating her song. Like other fairy-tale children, Benedetta took this miracle in stride. Instead of being awed by the unusual nature of the event, or thanking God for being witness to His power, she simply commanded the bird to stop singing because she did not want to be accompanied.[12] The nightingale obeyed and resumed his melody only when Benedetta allowed it. Over the next two years, the nightingale, most famous of birds for the quality of its nocturnal song, could be found singing at all hours of the day or night that Benedetta desired. Like the dog, the nightingale was not quite what he appeared to be. Concealed in the body of an animal, he was really a guardian angel sent by God to protect her.

Why God would choose such a delicate creature to help Benedetta fight a formidable opponent like the devil is somewhat puzzling, especially because in European folk culture and literature the nightingale was a symbol of carnal love, of the sensual side of life, through which the devil frequently worked his wiles.[13] Perhaps it is precisely because of this that he is most appropriate as God's instrument in Benedetta's life. By choosing to aid her with this particular creature out of all creation, God in effect signalled his blessing on this aspect of her existence. The world of the senses, of earthly love, of close ties to nature, these were all part of God's bounty. If Benedetta was attracted to them she was also embracing the world of God.

Yet this was the world she would have to give up. When Benedetta reached the age of nine, her parents fulfilled the vow made at her birth. One early spring day, when the chestnut trees and the vines were beginning to show the first signs of new bloom, her father brought her down the mountain path to the nearby town of Pescia to join a group of women dedicated to the religious life.

Benedetta later recalled her mother's parting words: "When
I left home to come to Pescia, my mother told me, 'Leave
me, who am your mother; I want you to take the Mother
of God as your mother because I have heard that those
girls have a Madonna. In all your needs I want you to go
to her as you would to me.' "[14]

As Benedetta and her father set off on the road, the
nightingale once more appeared and began to follow. About
a mile from Vellano, however, Benedetta turned to him,
saying: "Goodbye nightingale, I am going to Pescia and
leaving you." The nightingale flew off into the sky and
according to the villagers was never again heard in those
parts.[15]

CHAPTER TWO

The Convent

THE IMPACT OF Benedetta's journey down the mountain must be measured in psychic and cultural distance. The seven miles between Vellano and Pescia separated vastly different personal worlds and cultural geographies. Benedetta was not only leaving her parents, who had lavished on her the kind of attention reserved solely for an only child who was the special recipient of God's grace, but she was leaving the world of the mountains for that of the plains—the world of nature, where the inroads of civilization were as tenuous as the precariously perched walls of Vellano, for that of the plains, where new people, new ways of doing things, and new ways of thinking were daily transforming the lives of ordinary people. If in the Mediterranean world the planting of grapes and olives was roughly coterminous with the line of civilization, then Vellano was barely at the edge. Just above the town, the landscape gave way to forests of oak, chestnuts, and ilex. The hoe had never scratched the surface of that land. "The mountains," Fernand Braudel tells us, are "a world apart from civilizations, which are an urban and lowland achievement."[1] The two worlds, of course, were not totally isolated. There was a necessary, though intermittent, movement of people and trade between them. Benedetta Carlini thus was an added link in a very old chain. But if the process of communication and exchange was, in the long run, of mutual benefit to both worlds, it was nonetheless filled with apprehension and mistrust. The fears of the lowland people for those of the highlands would make themselves felt much later in Benedetta's life, as they had on many other occasions in which towns-people had to deal with their neighbors from the mountains. For her part, Benedetta's account of her journey to the plains, made years later, does not mention her fears, but one can well imagine the feelings of a nine-year-old mountain girl approaching the busy stir of a small town in the shadow of one of the great cultural centers of Europe.

Pescia, where she was headed, was a rapidly growing regional center for the Valdinievole, a varied agricultural area between Pistoia and Lucca. The town's population had increased at a rate that outpaced every other city or town in the sixteenth-century Florentine state, doubling in the course of the century to reach over six thousand inhabitants in 1590. Fueling this surge of new people was a transformation of the Pesciatine economy and society. What had been a backward and impoverished agricultural area, undistinguished from many others in the Florentine dominion during the fifteenth century, had become, by the time Bendetta first saw it, a thriving market town for commercial crops, primarily silk, wine, and olive oil, as well as a site for a small paper industry. These activities linked the Pesciatines with a large international network of trade and people and these links in turn had significant cultural repercussions. The latest fashions in art and literature as well as in the more mundane artifacts of everyday life began to make their way into Pescia and to transform not only the social fabric but the very appearance of the town. Out of the medieval shell there burst forth new shops, new Renaissance palaces, new churches, new convents—in short, a new town.[2]

This was a place receptive to innovation, a place where outsiders could make their mark. Yet the din and bustle of a busy town could also muffle a person's attempts to be recognized. At Vellano, both nature and her parents, and perhaps her neighbors too, had acknowledged Benedetta's distinctive status. In fairy-tale style, they readily accepted the various signs that God had singled her out above others for his divine favor. The urban environment, however, was more impersonal and would require a greater persistence and a different kind of effort. The life of the fairy-tale heroine would have to be transformed into the life of the saint.

Whether this transformation would succeed depended in large measure on the extent to which Benedetta could adapt to the rapidly changing religious world she was about to enter. The convents of Pescia, like so many others in late sixteenth-century Europe, were still in the midst of profound reforms that affected both the number and the character of religious institutions. Under the combined pressures of population growth and the increased religious fervor of the Catholic Reformation, the town's convents and monasteries were bursting at the seams. To accommodate the swelling throng of applicants to the religious life, the town's two convents, San Michele, which had been founded in the twelfth century, and Santa Chiara, built in the 1490s, were both enlarged in mid-sixteenth century. When this did not suffice, local officials created a new convent, Santa Maria Nuova. In addition, a small group of women, known locally as the Theatines, also began to lead a religious life in common with the hope of eventually obtaining papal perimission to form a full-fledged convent. Yet, despite all these measures, many girls were refused entrance to these institutions for lack of space. Although at the time that Benedetta was entering the religious life, the convents of Pescia accommodated close to two hundred females above age eight, worried officials noted that for every girl admitted three applicants had to be turned away. The unfortunate people of Pescia, as one observer once exclaimed, were still "rich only in the number of girls with no place to go." To reserve as many openings as possible for the needs of the local population, grand ducal officials finally ruled in 1598 that because the area in which Pescia was located, the Valdinievole, bordered on the state of Lucca and some of the girls entering Pesciatine convents came from there, none of the town's convents were to accept foreign girls, either as nuns or as servants to them (*converse*).[3]

Knowing the difficulty of gaining entrance into the older and more prestigious convents that catered to the daughters of the Pesciatine patriciate, Benedetta's parents directed their steps to the newest religious institution, the Theatines, where it would be easier, and certainly cheaper, to place their daughter. Getting a girl admitted into a convent involved careful social and financial planning. The hierarchically ordered social world that existed outside the convent walls penetrated the inside. The convent of Santa Maria Nuova, for instance, would only admit girls born of Pesciatine fathers who were eligible to hold public office.[4] In effect, this meant restricting the pool of applicants to wealthy property holders whose families had lived in the town for several generations.[5] But even if there had been no such rule, the networks of kinship, patronage, and association that existed on the outside influenced where a girl might be placed. A family was likely to put a girl in a convent where she already had a sister, cousin, or family friend. The idea was to strengthen from the inside the networks that already existed on the outside world. For similar reasons, since new girls were accepted into a convent by a vote of the nuns who were there, the latter would be inclined to accept the girls of their own families or of those that were close to them. A case in point were the nuns of the convent of San Michele of Pescia, who in 1612 petitioned the Grand Duke of Tuscany, Cosimo de' Medici II, to allow them to take in a *conversa* from Collodi, a town just outside the Florentine state. When Cosimo replied that they should look further for candidates from within Pesciatine territory, the nuns dutifully looked at five, voting down each one in turn. They then wrote back the grand duke, reiterating their request and adding that they liked the Collodi girl best of all because she excelled at working silk and because she was coming with a dowry of 100 scudi, twice the dowry of other *converse*. At that point the provost of Pescia, the highest ecclesiastical authority in the town, intervened with a report to Cosimo stating the real motivations behind the case. The girl in question was the daughter of Sister Jacopa, one of the oldest nuns at San Michele. The five Pesciatine girls the nuns had looked at did not stand a chance of getting in, the provost argued, because the nuns' vote had been partisan. On his recommendation, the nuns' petition was denied, making this one of the rare instances in which family interests did not triumph. Yet this was an unusual case and for that very reason the records for it survive in contrast to the routinely passed admissions that went unnoticed. What made this case unique was not really that Sister Jacopa had a daughter—many a widow with grown children had entered convents in the past—but rather that she was a convert from Judaism. By what strange path she ended up as a nun at San Michele, we do not know, but it does seem clear that a converted Jew could not bring the same pressure on the provost as a nun from a well-established Christian family. Still, kinship ties had been strong enough to persuade the majority of nuns in the convent to support the request and to appeal in its favor for well over a year.[6]

As this story suggests, not just kinship but money was

important in establishing a girl in a convent. The marriage market for a bride of Christ was tied to the marriage market for the brides of ordinary men. And in sixteenth-century Tuscany it was a buyer's market. Because men were increasingly postponing marriage or remaining single, the cost of dowries, whether secular or religious, grew. To find a husband for a wellborn Pesciatine girl at the close of the 1500s required a dowry of at least 1500 scudi; to place her in a prestigious convent like Santa Chiara took around 400 scudi. Little wonder that this was an attractive option for patrician families with an ample number of daughters and that Pescia's convents were flooded with applicants. Nonetheless, even 400 scudi were beyond the means of most people at a time when a skilled laborer earned no more than 55 or 60 scudi a year.[7] A girl of middling wealth, which in the context of Pesciatine society is all that Benedetta Carlini was, would have to find a cheaper institution.

The Theatine community of Pescia was attempting to develop just such a place. The dowries paid by entrants in the early seventeenth century varied considerably depending on the ability to pay, but averaged only 160 scudi. What accounted for this was that despite their name, the Theatines of Pescia were not really Theatines.[8] Indeed, in 1599, when Benedetta first joined them, they were not even full-fledged nuns in a regularly enclosed convent. The group had been formed nine years earlier by Piera Pagni, the widow of a prominent Pesciatine whose kinsmen were highly placed church and state officials. Together with a handful of young women, Piera founded a retreat in a private house where they all led a communal life engaged in prayer and spiritual exercises. The group supported itself with the dowries that each of the members brought with her and with the income derived from manual labor, which for them as for most Pesciatine women, consisted of making raw silk into thread for the Florentine silk cloth industry.[9]

The formation of religious communities like these was a common phenomenon in the last half of the sixteenth century. Occupying an intermediate place between the religious and the secular world, they provided an outlet for the religious fervor and social needs of women who could not or did not want to join already established convents. Their less stringent dowry requirements were related to their lack of prestige in comparison with regular convents and to the fact that their members took only a simple and easily dissolved vow of chastity, rather than the "solemn vows" of obedience, poverty, and chastity, which in the eyes of the Church could not be renounced. The precarious position of these communities made them less demanding financially for fear of not being able to attract prospective candidates or to coerce those already in them to remain. These concerns surfaced in 1619 when the Pope asked the Theatines to pay a tax to the papacy. Pirro Torrigiani, one of their administrators, wrote back saying that they could not possibly pay because "all they have is what they earned with their labor and their dowries. And even though they have been in a congregation in a private house and engaged in good works, with the intention of building a monastery, they nonetheless did not submit to the jurisdiction of the Church; neither did they bind themselves to remain in their retreat and congregation, so that there are those who have left and took with them that which they brought."[10]

Financial considerations, and the abandonment of the religious life by some, while very real problems, however, should not obscure the religious commitment of such congregations. Some of the most devout and successful religious orders for women, the Ursulines among others, started from such modest origins. They did so, not be-

cause their foundresses could not afford to join other institutions, but rather because their strong religious vocation could not be fulfilled in the often corrupt world of
well-established convents, where the life led by the discarded daughters of patrician families was in many ways
undistinguishable from the life of the upper classes on
the outside.[11]

Undoubtedly, many convents had undergone internal
reform since 1563, when the Council of Trent issued new
decrees concerning the government of convents and ordered the full enclosure of all nuns regardless of any
privileges they had enjoyed up to that time. But, despite
the aid of secular governments, which might be persuaded to cooperate because the purity of convents was
thought crucial to the welfare of all society, such rules
were hard to implement. Even in the Florentine state,
reform was slow notwithstanding the Medici duke's deep
concern with convent life even before Trent, when he
appointed small secular boards (*operai*) to oversee the
administration of every convent in the state and prohibited lay people from going in and out of convents at will.[12]
In 1558, thirteen years after the enactment of the such
laws, Cosimo de' Medici wrote to Cardinal Guido Ascanio
Sforza:

> And to be brief, I tell you that one of the great cares I have
> in this world is to preserve the honor of God with regard
> to these convents. There have always been a few of bad
> repute and an infinite number of very holy and religious
> ones; because of affairs of war, I haven't been able to attend
> to them promptly; some of those that used to lead a bad
> life and which through my diligence lifted themselves up
> from it have returned to the mire and in some, where I
> have vigorously intervened, I have found more than 15
> nuns violated and because of this I have detained some of
> the leading gentlemen of this city; in some I have found
> more and in others less. . . . I have found that priests

and friars are the worst violators, although there are also others.[13]

At Pescia in the 1580s and 1590s, such goings-on were not unknown. The nuns of Santa Chiara, for example, had often been seen socializing with the Franciscan friars who were supposed to minister to their spiritual needs but who found occasion to offer other types of consolation. The nuns and the friars exchanged packages and letters regularly despite the efforts of the Pesciatine city council to put an end to such behavior. Matters reached a head when in 1610, under orders of the provost, the *operai* of Santa Chiara hid in the church of the convent and captured two of the roaming friars. This was "followed by a great riot and a gathering of people and by a great uprising of the nuns." The *operai* scuffled with the friars, pulling one by the nose, while the nuns retaliated by throwing stones and bricks at them. The affair reached the ears of the grand duke when the nuns of Santa Chiara wrote to him protesting their mistreatment and asking him to appoint another set of *operai*. Of the four they had, one, they complained, "is riddled by gout and is always in bed"; another "is a decrepit old man and cannot function"; and a third "is able-bodied but doesn't want to put himself out." The grand duke was not very receptive. Instead of complying with their request, he pressured the provincial superior of the Franciscans to remove the two friars, who were promptly dispatched to a three-year exile in Corsica.[14]

If the authorities expected that the removal of the two friars would significantly alter life at the convent, they must have been greatly vexed by subsequent events. The nuns and the remaining friars continued their activities for another decade, at least. In 1621, word spread in the town that one of the local shoemakers had just been given to repair a rather odd pair of wooden clogs. Inside one was carved a "nefarious figure unfit even for a public brothel," and written under it were the words, "for my good" (*Del mio bene*). Inside the other was a piece of white wood "in the form of a male sexual organ *al naturale*." Upon making inquiries about it, local officials discovered that the clogs were brought to the shoemaker by the housekeeper of the nuns of Santa Chiara. When they summoned her to appear before them she testified that she had received them from one of the nuns. The nun, in turn, claimed that the pieces of wood were made by one of the friars for the purpose of covering up a hole. At this point, city officials realized that more drastic measures were needed to solve the problem. They obtained permission from the grand duke to write Rome asking that the Franciscan friars be permanently barred from the convent and that they be replaced with more worthy spiritual guides.[15]

It is against this kind of corruption and in the context of a strong commitment to a reformed post-Tridentine church that we must understand the founding of the Theatines at Pescia. Piera Pagni, the patrician widow who organized the Theatines, could have entered any number of religious institutions. She had the wealth and the social standing to be accepted either at San Michele, Santa Maria Nuova, or Santa Chiara. But for someone with a strong religious vocation, life in the convents of Pescia would have been intolerably lax. If Piera Pagni was going to lead a truly religious life away from the vice and the material concerns of the secular world, she would have to found her own religious community.

The inspiration for this idea must have come from the example set by one of her kinsmen, Antonio Pagni, who in 1588 founded an independent religious congregation for men. Antonio, who had just obtained a degree in canon law at the University of Pisa, was joined by Father Paolo Ricordati, a former lawyer, and several other priests and laymen. Because of their reputation for saintliness, local people soon began to call them the Theatine fathers, after the Theatine Order of Clerics Regular, founded in 1524 by St. Cajetan Thiene to reform the Church. The label stuck with them even after they began to call themselves Fathers of the Holy Annunciation, and the label soon was extended to the female community founded by Piera Pagni when the male "Theatines" agreed to back them and provide spiritual direction.[16]

From the beginning, the female Theatines intended to become a regular monastic community. They set about it by leading a quasi-monastic existence under the spiritual direction of their father confessor, Paolo Ricordati, who urged them to adopt the so called Rule of St. Augustine. The Rule was not exactly a formal prescription for the regulation of their daily lives or the governance of the community but simply a set of spiritual counsels within which more specific rules could be accommodated by individual communities. It touched on such topics as the need to lead a communal life with no private property, the observance of prayers, the mortification of the flesh through fasts, the need for modest dress, and so on.[17] The rigor of the daily routine worked out under these guidelines can only be glimpsed fleetingly, since the actual constitution of the Theatines does not survive, and in any event was not written down until the 1650s for fear that a detailed account of their observances might deter prospective applicants from joining.[18] One of the Fathers of the Holy Annunication, however, left us a brief description of some of their observances, which consisted of "fasts, mortifications of the flesh, obedience, lessons, attendance at the Holy Sacraments every week, remaining secluded and letting themselves be seen only at Mass in the nearest church, confessing their sins in the refectory and every fifteen days at their place of prayer in the presence of all of them."[19] Interspersed with these spiritual exercises, several hours were set aside each day for man-

ual labor working silk. Such work was meant to instill
humility, discourage idleness, and raise revenues for the
community. To ensure that all the members complied with
these tasks and to help keep order, the Theatines created
a hierarchy of authority. "They have among themselves
a female superior under whom they govern themselves, a
teacher of the novices, and other customary offices as if
they were full-fledged nuns."[20]

At the same time that they organized themselves in-
ternally, they also set in motion the bureaucratic machin-
ery to legitimize their position within the Church. Having
shown that they could support themselves with the income from their dowries, their work, and a farm they
bought in 1610, they received permission from Rome the
following year to organize a general chapter and accept
new girls into their midst.[21] Apparently this bolstered
their ability to attract new applicants and financing, for
in April 1613 they asked the secular authorities for permission to build a monastery large enough to accommodate up to thirty women. At the moment they had no
more than eighteen members, but they were confident of
continuing growth. The project they proposed would cost
4000 scudi, part of which was for dismantling a section
of the city wall in order to make way for the building.
Located on a hillside with a superb view of the town and
the Pescia river valley, the finished project, completed in
October 1618, was impressive evidence of what a small
band of determined women could accomplish in a very
short time.[22]

Once settled in their new quarters, the Theatines began
the final round of administrative procedures to become a
regular convent. In 1619 they asked the pope to grant
them complete enclosure. No longer would they have to
go outside their convent to hear Mass, but more important, as nuns, their vows of poverty, chastity, and obedience would become solemn vows. Any nun wishing to

leave the convent could be constrained to stay by her superiors and by the secular authorities. Similarly, any laypersons trying to enter the convent without permission could also be punished.[23]

When the papal officials who handled such petitions received the Theatines' request, they asked the provost of Pescia to send in a report about them. The provost must have written favorably since in July of 1620, he and the Vicar of Pescia made one last visit to the convent to conclude the enclosure. Finally, on July 28, 1620, Pope Paul V issued the bull that made them a fully enclosed convent. According to the nuns' wishes, it was called the Congregation of the Mother of God and would be under the protection of St. Catherine of Siena. Their abbess, elected by the nuns from among themselves and approved by the provost of Pescia, was Benedetta Carlini.[24]

That a mountain girl from Vellano should reach such an eminent position is rather unusual. That she should do so at age thirty is even more so since the Council of Trent ruled that abbesses should be over forty years old whenever feasible. That she accomplished all this, moreover, while helping to steer the convent through the last stages of a complex bureaucratic process that was crucial to its institutional survival is nothing short of remarkable.[25] Yet these events, as we will see, were probably not unrelated. The rising fortunes of the Congregation of the Mother of God may have been closely linked to the rising fortunes of Benedetta Carlini and to the extraordinary claims that she made for both.

CHAPTER THREE

The Nun

BENEDETTA'S FIRST YEARS with the Theatines, after her arrival in 1599, were outwardly unremarkable. Looking back on that period twenty years later, the rest of the community remembered that "after she entered the house and lived among the other girls she was always very obedient and exemplary in all her actions. She never did anything worthy of rebuke and she took communion twice a week." Only Benedetta was aware of the supernatural events that were beginning to unfold.

As soon as her father left her, Benedetta did as her mother had told her when they parted at Vellano. Kneeling in front of the convent's statue of the Madonna, the nine-year-old girl sought her protection: "My most sweet Mother, I have left my carnal mother for you, I beg you to take me as your daughter." The Madonna seemed to nod her assent.

Not long after this, she again indicated that her adopted daughter was particularly dear to her. "One time when I was saying certain prayers in front of her image and I did not know what to meditate on that would please both her and me, as a sign that she was pleased, my mother leaned over the small altar." Benedetta thought that the Virgin

wanted to kiss her but she was so frightened by the movement of the statue that she fled in panic as it fell over the
altar. "I began to scream. I called the Mother Superior,
who ran over and set her straight."

Benedetta's reaction to the Virgin's gesture stands in
marked contrast to her earlier responses to supernatural
events. Whereas before she had accepted miracles as being
in the nature of things, now she was astounded and awed
by them. The actions of the Virgin testified to the mighty
power of God. Like the miracles of the saints, which the
girls in the convent read to strengthen their religious faith,
what Benedetta witnessed was not something to absorb
but to think about and learn from.[1] Her childhood and
childish faith were giving way to the religious world of
the adult. Folk culture was being replaced by religious
culture. The fairy-tale heroine was beginning to follow in
the footsteps of the saints.

Because of fear, Benedetta did not tell the mother superior or anyone else in the community about everything
she saw at the altar that day. Instead, she simply said
that the Virgin had fallen—news that was received as
unfortunate but not catastrophic. Eventually, Benedetta
persuaded herself of the same thing. The fall of a holy
image could, of course, have a variety of meanings. It
could signify divine favor, as Benedetta had first thought;
it could be a bad omen, or it could be merely a natural
accident with no great significance. Insofar as they thought
about it, the Theatines interpreted the event in a somewhat negative light, but mostly they viewed it as unremarkable. Although it was remembered and retold several
decades later, no lasting importance seems to have been
attached to it at the time. Benedetta quickly returned to
the obscurity of communal life.[2]

There was less ambiguity and certainly more notoriety
about the supernatural events that began to occur in 1613,
just before the Theatines received permission to build

their convent. Benedetta, now a young woman of twenty-three, reported to her mother superior and to her father confessor that she was seeing visions. The first occurred one morning while she was praying. Suddenly she felt herself to be in a beautiful garden with many fruits and flowers. In the center was a fountain with scented water, and next to it was an angel, holding a sign with gold letters: "Whosoever wants to take water from this fountain, let him purge his cup or not come nearer." Because she did not understand the meaning of the sign, she asked the angel. He explained, "If you want to know God, lift all earthly desires from your heart." On hearing these words, Benedetta felt a strong urge to take leave of the world, but, instead, the vision ceased, and with great inner wrenching she returned to the normal world of the senses. Afterward she felt great happiness and a stronger desire than ever to be good.[3]

Later that same year, she saw herself surrounded by a pack of wild animals—lions, scorpions, and boars—who wanted to harm her. At the last possible moment she was saved by a man dressed in great splendor who made the animals go away. He said he was Jesus and the animals were demons she would have to battle. He encouraged her to be strong and told her he would always come to her aid. Then he disappeared.[4]

In another vision, a young boy of nine or ten took her to the base of a mountain and told her to climb to the top. Because the terrain was difficult, she stumbled, falling repeatedly to a lower point. Finally, he took her by the hand and led her to the top. Once there, he said to her, "Thus you will never be able to climb the Mount of Perfection without the true guide on which to lean." When she asked him who that might be, he answered, "your father confessor."[5]

The content of mystical experiences, whether we view them as psychological or divine revelations, or as phys-

iological responses to fasting, discloses the mystic's deep-
est spiritual concerns. To understand the messages revealed in Benedetta's visions is therefore to understand
what was foremost in her mind. Although manifested in
a variety of ways, the underlying theme of her early visions was always the same: the spiritual world is superior
to the material; one must give up the one in order to
attain the other; the road is difficult and beset by dangers
but these can be overcome with divine guidance; although
human beings are frail creatures, if they are willing to
engage in the struggle for perfection, God in his mercy
will help them.

That a young woman leading a monastic life should
hear words of this sort is not surprising. Seeking to become a better nun, Benedetta undoubtedly found the road
to spiritual perfection arduous. The figures she saw in
her visions simply acknowledged the difficulties she faced
and at the same time gave her courage and hope for the
future.

To point this out is neither to diminish the spiritual
reality of these experiences for Benedetta nor to suggest
that only the final message, rather than the visions themselves, is important. The specific manifestations of the
message received are as significant for understanding the
visionary experience as is the general meaning derived
from them by the visionary. Because visions encapsule
the social and cultural experiences of the visionary, they
must be understood in their concrete details as well as in
their underlying purpose. This is especially true of the
visions of pre-modern European mystics, who lived in a
culture that taught a particularly visual form of mental
prayer.

When Benedetta tells us that "she did not know what
to meditate on" while she was praying, she had in mind
a specific type of meditation involving a sophisticated
ability to visualize those people, places, and events in the

life of the Holy Family that were appropriate for certain
types of prayer. Like other girls of her day, she had been
taught to do this through one of the many popular handbooks printed for this purpose, such as Luis de Granada's
Manual of Prayers and Spiritual Exercises or St. Charles Borromeo's book on prayer, which the Theatines owned and
which Benedetta occasionally read. These books commonly recommended:

> The better to impress the story of the Passion in your mind,
> and to memorize each action of it more easily, it is helpful
> and necessary to fix the places and people in your mind:
> a city, for example, which will be the city of Jerusalem—
> taking for this purpose a city that is well known to you.
> In this city find the principal places in which all the epi-
> sodes of the Passion would have taken place. . . . And
> then too you must shape in your mind some people, people
> well known to you, to represent for you the people in-
> volved in the Passion. . . .
> When you have done all this, putting all your imagina-
> tion into it, then go into your chamber. Alone and solitary,
> excluding every external thought from your mind, start
> thinking of the beginning of the Passion, starting with how
> Jesus entered Jerusalem on the ass. Moving slowly from
> episode to episode, meditate on each one, dwelling on each
> single stage and step of the story. . . .[6]

It is this kind of literature that gave rise to some of the
particular features of Benedetta's visions. Although when
questioned about them by her superiors, Benedetta claimed
that there were no outward sources for what she saw, it
is clear from her answers that she had assimilated the
devotional literature she had read and heard. She recalled,
for instance, that before she saw the vision of the Mount
of Perfection, she had been listening to a certain book
that was read out loud to all the nuns, and that the book
discussed how to deal with the sins and defects of one's
past life. She had not intended, she said, to climb to the

top of the Mount, but "she had read about it many times along with the other girls in a book that deals with the highest level of perfection in the three vows taken by religious [monks and nuns], and in particular, having read that he who wants to climb the Mount of Perfection, has to exert himself."[7]

In addition to reading literary manuals on prayer and other devotional literature, the nuns in Benedetta's convent sought to attain a higher level of prayer by creating interior images based on paintings and sculptures they had seen in real life. As the art historian Michael Baxandall has pointed out, in the Renaissance and early modern period, "the painter was a professional visualizer of the holy stories." He gave outward form to what the devout had already begun to represent in their own minds and his function was to stimulate them further in their inner devotions.[8] Nothing is more natural then than to hear Benedetta exclaim that the figure of St. Catherine of Siena, which appeared in one of her visions, "was dressed just as one sees her in the paintings."[9] Benedetta would have seen such images in the parish church at Vellano or in some of the churches of Pescia where the Theatines attended Mass and received the sacrament before they became an enclosed convent.

Similarly, despite Benedetta's disclaimer to having seen or read about a garden like the one in her first vision, she was undoubtedly inspired by both literary and pictorial sources. Her vision echoes the biblical tale of the woman of Samaria. When Jesus approached the well from which the woman was drawing water, he told her that "whosoever drinketh of the water that I shall give him shall never thirst" (John 4:14). Yet the garden where Benedetta heard the angel's words also recalls another episode in the life of the Holy Family—an episode among the most popular in the iconography of late medieval and Renaissance art. With its profusion of beautiful flowers, its young angel with gold and white wings, its fountain, and its divine message emblazoned in gold letters, the secluded garden in which she found herself resembles the garden of the Annunciation. The enclosed garden, a symbol of the virginity of Mary, the fountain, representing the well of life from which came spiritual rebirth, the banner of the "Hail Mary," all of these had become staples of the pictorial vocabulary of the time. If Benedetta did not recall having seen such images outside of her own mind, this surely was because she had successfully internalized the religious discourse of her society.[10]

Despite the conventional imagery and uplifting tone of her visions, Benedetta reacted to them with mixed emotions. Like other visionaries, she was aware of the power and danger of visions. Living as a believer in a profoundly religious society, she did not question the reality of visions. The modern tendency to view such phenomena as pathological hallucinations had not yet emerged. The problem was not whether the visions were real or not, but whether they were diabolical or heavenly in origin. What made it difficult to determine was that in order to ensnare his unsuspecting victim, the devil adopted different guises, many of them seemingly good. By appearing handsome and uttering virtuous words, he could bring the devout over to his side and then use them to do his evil deeds. St. Paul had cautioned the pious, "Satan himself is transformed into an angel of light" (2 Cor. 11), and numerous treatises written for the spiritual direction of nuns and priests in the intervening centuries continued to warn them of their vulnerability when they abandoned themselves to mystical encounters with the supernatural. Their very devoutness could be used against them by the enemy of God.[11]

Initially, Benedetta feared that this might be happening to her. Upon hearing Jesus tell her that he would always be with her, "she felt fear. . . . And those words made me wonder about a diabolical illusion." Similarly, when she found herself alone in the garden with the fountain, "she felt terror."[12] Yet, the fear and trepidation experienced at the start always gave way gradually to feelings of great happiness and contentment. "And coming out of her prayer, it seemed to her that she was totally content and happy, with greater desire than before to be good, and she felt in love with Jesus." Thus, "at the start of the visions she was afraid, wondering if they were from the devil or from God, but afterwards, slowly, slowly she felt reassured."[13] Her emotional journey through fear, acceptance, and happiness mirrors that of other mystics before her, and this knowledge in itself provided consolation. It was a journey rooted in the gamut of emotions first experienced by the Mother of God, whose fear when she heard that the Lord had singled her out above all other women turned to acceptance and then to joy.

Benedetta's growing confidence in the divine provenance of her visions, though never absolute, was bolstered by the feelings of happiness she experienced. In her age, as in ours, emotions were charged with meaning, but whereas in the twentieth century emotions are perceived as the result of experience, the final internal product of external events, in the seventeenth century they were still considered experience itself; they gave meaning and shape to events; they validated moral truths. Feelings of happiness were of divine origin; fear and terror came from the devil. Consequently, as moralists since the early days of the Church observed,

> the presence either of good from evil spirits by the help of God can easily be distinguished. The vision of the holy ones is not fraught with distraction. . . . But it comes so quietly and gently that immediately joy, gladness and courage arise in the soul. . . . Yet if, being men, some fear the vision of the good, those who appear immediately take fear away. . . . But the inroads and the display of the evil spirits

is fraught with confusion, with din, with sounds and cryings
. . . from which arise fear in the heart, tumult and confusion
of thought, dejection. . . . Whenever, therefore, ye have
seen ought and are afraid, if your fear is immediately taken
away and in place of it comes joy unspeakable, cheerful-
ness, courage, renewed strength, calmness of thought
. . . boldness and love toward God, take courage and pray.
For joy and a settled state of the soul show the holiness of
him who is present. But if at the appearance of any there
is confusion, knocking without, wordly display, threats of
death . . . know ye that it is an onslaught of evil spirits.[14]

To test the legitimacy of her visions, Benedetta sub-
jected her emotions to constant scrutiny. She became acutely
conscious of the slightest change in her emotional state.
As added protection, however, she also told her superiors
about her experiences. In doing this she was merely following the advice given her by her supernatural guide on
the Mount of Perfection—i.e., to lean on her confessor as
her spiritual counselor.

On hearing the content of her visions, Benedetta's confessor and the abbess did not discount the importance of
her emotions. Neither did they doubt that she had experienced visions since some of them had occurred in the
presence of witnesses who had observed that during prayer
she had gone into a trance-like state in which she gesti-
culated and made incomprehensible sounds. During these
episodes, her altered state of consciousness had made it
impossible for her companions to receive answers to their
anxious queries about what was happening to her. Thus
while the public setting of her visions had already helped
to corroborate Benedetta's claims, her account now provided her superiors with an insider's explanation for the
events that others had seen.[15]

Yet the question remained: were these visions diabolical
or were they divine in origin? The Church had always
found revelation and personal mysticism problematic. Vi-

sions were accepted as one of the ways in which God guided human beings to salvation and over the centuries, the visions of the saints were written down and used by preachers as evidence of the truths of Christianity and as moral exhortations for the devout.[16] Nonetheless, despite their theological grounding and their pedagogical value, visions were increasingly looked on with suspicion because they remained outside the sacramental structure of the Church. Normally, communication between the devout and God was mediated by clerics through the administration of the sacraments. In the sixteenth century, especially, when the ecclesiastical hierarchy was coming under attack both from within the Church and from Protestant dissidents, efforts were undertaken to curb all forms of charismatic experiences that bypassed clerical intervention. The aim of these efforts was to weaken all competing conduits for grace and to limit the propagation of heresy by well meaning but ignorant visionaries whose flawed interpretations of their experiences could inadvertently lead them and their followers into doctrinal errors. Without exception, the mystics of the sixteenth century, some of them on their way to becoming the great saints of the Catholic Church, were questioned at length until most doubts about the genuineness, the divine provenance, and the orthodoxy of their visions could be laid to rest.[17]

The visions of female mystics were, moreover, probed with greater zeal than those of men. Already in the fifteenth century, the theologian Jean Gerson had warned that the visions and sayings of women were "to be held suspect unless carefully examined, and much more fully than men's . . . because they are easily seduced."[18] Women did not have the reasoning powers of men; they were the "weaker vessel," whose limited mental capacities, unbridled curiosity, and insatiable lusts made them easy prey to the snares of the devil.[19] Paradoxically, women's propensity to credulity and to simple faith, which swelled their ranks among the accepted mystics of late medieval and early modern Europe and which, in the eyes of contemporaries, gave them an advantage over men in attaining a close union with God, also often made them the unwitting instruments of the devil.[20]

With this in mind, Benedetta's confessor told her to disbelieve anything she saw so as not to give the devil grounds on which to work his tricks. To believe oneself elected by God for special grace could be an act of supreme vanity, and the devil knew how to use such thoughts to his advantage. Father Ricordati counselled her to try to repress the onset of visions and to "pray to God that He send her travails instead of ecstasies and revelations, since it seemed to her that this would be safer against the deceits of the devil."[21] The call for travails would be an act of penitence that would help Benedetta expiate her pride. It would also teach her humility, a particularly desirable virtue in a nun. By asking Benedetta to follow his advice, he hoped it would be more difficult for the devil to appeal to Benedetta's sense of vanity. One of the signs of a true seer was the feeling of unworthiness, of not meriting God's grace. What better way to show this than to ask God for physical suffering? Many female saints had undertaken such penitence and had been blessed with debilitating ailments that allowed them to exercise both their humility and their unstinting devotion to God.[22]

Since obedience was one of the most important attributes of a good nun, Benedetta did as she was told. She struggled to keep from having visions and apparently succeeded, but she had greater difficulty in receiving some sort of travail. Her prayers were not answered until 1615, when she finally began to experience such intense pains over her entire body, especially at night, that she was often paralyzed by them. The physicians who were called in to examine her were baffled by her illness. They could neither diagnose it nor determine what to do. None of the remedies they tried eased her pain.[23]

Benedetta's illness may be more understandable to us than to her physicians. The deep sense of conflict between her natural inclination to give in to ecstatic experiences and her desire to follow the advice of her confessor weighed very heavily on her mind. Despite her own initial doubts, she wanted desperately to believe that her visions were good, that they were of divine origin and that they exalted her. But she was told they might be evil; that to be an obedient nun, which she very much wanted to be, she would have to give up the very things she most wanted. There was no easy way to resolve the difficulty. If she denied the visions, she might be denying God; if she accepted them, she might be helping the devil. "The greatest battle she had," she commented years later, "was to not want to believe that it was God . . . and this gave her great pain, because His Excellency [the provost] came here and said she should not believe [in her visions] and she felt she could not do anything but to believe, and she tested herself; she prayed to God that he take that belief away from her, yet the belief grew stronger; she felt pain at not being able to obey him and the pain would go away only because she couldn't think about it anymore or she would have gone mad."[24]

Benedetta's malady was a physical manifestation of the internal suffering and the unresolved conflict she was experiencing. But, at the same time, it was the first step toward some relief. Illness was the only acceptable solution to her dilemma because it implicitly placed her on the side of God. This was the sign of divine favor that Paolo Ricordati, her confessor, had asked for. This was the answer to her prayers and a validation of Jesus' statement that she would have to undergo many tribulations for love of him. Like other female mystics before her, she was following the path that led to holiness.[25]

Yet, if Benedetta expected recognition from others for being the recipient of extraordinary grace, she was to be sadly disappointed. To be sure, doctors were called in to examine her, but they departed rather quickly when they found they could not help her. Benedetta was left to deal with her pain by herself. The life of the nuns returned to its uninterrupted rounds of prayer, fasts, and manual work, and Benedetta receded from the limelight as her visions gave way to an illness for which nothing could be done. For two years she suffered quietly in the obscurity of communal life.

Matters took another turn in 1617, when her visions resumed. But these were not a simple return to the ecstasies and revelations she had experienced before the onset of her ailment. Instead of encounters with Jesus and with benevolent angels, she now was pursued at night by handsome young men who wanted to kill her and who beat her all over with iron chains, swords, sticks, and other weapons. The attacks took place several times a week after going to bed and lasted for six to eight hours. They were accompanied by excruciating physical pain.

Not content with their assaults on her body, the youths also tried to corrupt her soul. They urged her to come with them and leave the Theatines, telling her that by persevering in her monastic life she would only make herself ill without, in the final analysis, being certain of her own salvation. Their leader in particular, whom she recognized as someone she had seen in the streets of Pescia, was especially eager to lead her astray. At first he approached her with words of endearment, hoping to seduce her by his feigned gentleness. He asked her to be his bride and even showed her a ring, which he wanted to put on her finger as a seal of their bond. She replied that she would rather be ill in the monastery for love of Jesus than to go with him, adding, "I would like to be the bride of Christ, not yours." These words so angered him that he tried to put the ring on her by force. In the struggle he revealed his true nature. His gentleness gave way to rage, his beautiful face became hideous, and he beat her with a savagery unmatched by his followers.[26]

Whenever the young men appeared, Benedetta tried to avoid temptation by not looking at them directly. She would also make the sign of the cross to protect herself, but this only made them angrier and they would attack her with greater zeal. Occasionally, she overcame her reluctance to disturb the sleep of the other nuns and called for help. These cries finally alerted her superiors to the seriousness of Benedetta's plight and they assigned her a young companion, Bartolomea Crivelli, to help her in her battles with the devil. Bartolomea was to share Benedetta's cell and to keep an eye on her at all times. Later, the convent's superiors would have reason to regret this measure, which unwittingly provided Benedetta with the means to act out her erotic visions. But it would be several years before they found this out. In the meantime, what they knew was limited to what Benedetta told them and what they could observe of her nightly struggles with their own eyes. Their convent was graced by the presence of a mystic whose body was the battleground for supernatural forces. The assignment of Bartolomea as Benedetta's companion was a tacit acknowledgment of Benedetta's assertions.

If at this point the confessor and the mother superior had any further concerns about the validity of Benedetta's claims, they did not voice them. On the contrary, they became extremely solicitous of her welfare and because of her weakened condition, excused her from participation in many of the daily routines of the community. After all, if Benedetta was a true visionary, then the convent was privileged to have her; by virtue of her divine election, the entire community had a share in her glory. God had not only chosen Benedetta as His special handmaiden, but had made the convent itself an object of divine favor. This notion, which was voiced openly in the next few years, could be used to bolster the convent's own claims for special recognition.[27] In 1618, as the construction of their spacious new building was coming to a close and they began to plan the next steps for becoming a regular convent, what better proof of their worthiness could they offer than the presence of a holy woman in their midst? Surely, Pope Paul V would grant their request for full enclosure.

Indeed, as the day for the solemn procession to their new quarters arrived, Benedetta walked in an ecstatic trance, seeing the angels of Pescia paying homage to her and scattering flowers along her path, as if she were the image of St. Dorothy, the patron saint of Pescia, being paraded in its annual procession through town. Once they arrived at the gates of the convent, the Madonna greeted her and gave her and her companion two guardian angels.[28]

We can be certain that the ecstatic nun who acknowledged the homage of the angels and smiled and gestured toward the Virgin did not go unnoticed among the townsfolk. Quite a few people would have turned out for the procession, not just to break up the monotony of their daily lives, but because religious processions were important events in any town. The ritual space they delineated linked the communal topography to a sacred order. Customarily, the processional routes, the order in which the participants walked, the prayers and chants recited, and the stops made along important places on the way, all these were matters to be taken up by the highest levels of local church and government administration.[29] If in the course of one of these ceremonies the Virgin appeared to a participant, as she had forty years earlier on Pescia's main bridge, the spot where the vision occurred could become a pilgrimage center, drawing people by the hundreds.[30] News of Benedetta's trance probably traveled quickly and that evening must have been the subject of gossip around most Pesciatine hearths.

The fact that no one other than Benedetta could actually

see the flowers and angels along the way was likely of little significance to most people. Although signs could help to corroborate the truth of visions, they were not absolutely necessary. In any event, what the devout deemed a sufficient sign in the seventeenth century differed from our own notions. For many contemporaries, both among laypersons and theologians, the rapture of the visionary was in itself an indication that a direct channel of communication with heaven had been established. Yet already in the seventeenth century the standards of proof were becoming more stringent. Increasingly, seers and visionaries were asked to show verifiable signs—tangible evidence outside of their own psychic state.[31] For the doubting Thomases that may have wanted such signs from Benedetta, there soon was something to dispel their skepticism. Three months after the Theatines were installed in their new quarters, on the second Friday of Lent, Benedetta received the stigmata:

> While I was in bed between two and three at night the thought came to me to suffer the things suffered by Jesus Christ, and while I was of this mind a crucifix, with a living man crucified on it appeared, and he asked whether I wanted to suffer for love of him, who was Jesus Christ. But before I could ask him: "but what if this were an illusion of the Devil? If this were so, I am not willing to consent. I would like my spiritual father to know these things"; he made the sign of the cross on my heart. Once this was done, the crucified man told me that this was not an illusion of the devil but that he was God, and that he wanted that I suffer for the duration of my life, and therefore that I arrange myself in the form of the Cross because he wanted to imprint his holy wounds on my body. I arranged myself in the form of the Cross as he ordered, and at that moment a flash burst from all the wounds of that crucifix that was in front of me and it seemed to me that those rays that he had in his wounds imprinted themselves in my hands, feet, and side of my chest. And on his head I saw many rays, but small ones, which seemed to me to surround my head

and I felt tremendous pain in my hands, feet, side, and head. But then in the same instant there came such contentment to my heart that never in my life have I felt anything like it, and he said that I should prepare myself to suffer until my death and that he wanted that I resemble him in all things, adding that I should tell my spiritual father exactly everything, as I did.[32]

This miraculous event was witnessed by Bartolomea Crivelli, Benedetta's companion, who as usual, kept her company in her room to help her with her nightly travails. She not only heard Benedetta's exchange with Christ, but was the first to see the signs on her body:

> I was present when she received those signs . . . and I saw that she arranged herself in the form of the Cross and became as red as a glowing ember and she said, "My Lord, there are others who are better than me, I don't deserve this since I am a sinner." And I could see that she suffered such pain on her hands, feet, and side, and remaining like this a little while, she asked that I lift her by the arm because she couldn't do it by herself. And I lifted her and saw that she had some red marks like small rosettes on her hands, feet, and side, and she had a deep red band around her head, but it was bloodless. And then I left, but in any case I was there and pretended not to pay any attention to her.[33]

From that moment Benedetta was no longer neglected by the nuns. To receive the stigmata was no ordinary event, even in the seventeenth century. It was one thing to have visions: in an era of intense religious revival, these were not too unusual. But to receive the holy wounds of Christ was a miracle of a different order of magnitude. The stigmata did not have to be accepted on the basis of faith but could be verified by one's senses. Everyone could perceive them, even those most anchored to the realities of everyday existence.

Benedetta was quickly given the earthly recognition to

match her heavenly grace. Sometime between February and May, 1619, the Theatine nuns elected her to be their abbess. Presumably this was done with the customary approval of their father confessor, who heard from Benedetta herself about how she received the stigmata. Father Ricordati also began to visit the convent regularly during the Lenten season to hear her give sermons to the other nuns while they purified themselves with their whips as part of their penance. As she talked to them, Benedetta was always in a trance and spoke, not as herself, but as an angel who exhorted the nuns to lead a better life. The angel usually ended the sermons by praising Benedetta, chosen above all others to receive the signs of God's grace.

Had Benedetta not been in an altered state of consciousness, Father Ricordati would not have allowed her to give sermons. Since the early days of the Church, women had been barred from speaking in the house of God as well as preaching, teaching, or speaking in public: "As in all the churches of the saints," wrote St. Paul, "wives should keep silence in the churches. They are not permitted to speak, but should be subordinate, as even the law says. If there is anything they desire to know, let them ask their husbands at home. For it is shameful for a woman to speak in church."[34] This prohibition grew out of the synthesis of separate traditions, the Greek, which taught that women were by nature inferior to men and therefore should be their subordinates,[35] and the Biblical, which suggested to many readers that women be perpetually silent as a punishment for the sins of Eve, whose garrulousness brought disaster to all mankind. "The curse of God pronounced on your sex weighs still on the world. Guilty you must bear its hardships," wrote Tertullian in the third century. "You are the devil's gateway . . . you softened up with your cajoling words the man against whom the devil could not prevail by force."[36] Over the centuries these themes hardened until silence became a virtue particularly recommended to women. "By silence, indeed, women achieve the fame of eloquence," wrote one Renaissance commentator.[37] Of course, a handful of women were, in principle, allowed to achieve eloquence by more conventional means: those who ruled, those who managed to acquire unusual learning despite the barriers to female education, and those who fell into a trance. Yet the exceptional nature of these women, and the grudging acceptance they received, is underscored again and again by the comments of their male contemporaries. Peter Martyr Vermigli (1500–1562), for instance, admits that "it is not to be denied that some women imbued with the gift of prophecy have taught the people in public, passing on to them those things which were revealed to them by God. For divine gifts are not conferred in order to be hidden away, but so that they may promote the edification of the Church as a whole. But it should not be deduced from this that that which God does in some particular case of privilege should be made by us a model of behavior."[38]

Benedetta's trances thus put her in the category of privileged women. They gave her a voice denied to her sisters, but one that was recognized as legitimate by her contemporaries.[39] She had not only achieved recognition, but had gained a public forum, especially since the convent was not yet fully enclosed and laypersons still had access to it. She had attained all this while remaining in compliance with the male-dominated values and social structure of her age. The content of her mysticism repeatedly stressed obedience to her confessor and her sermons had received his tacit approval.

Satisfied with her orthodoxy, Father Ricordati allowed Benedetta to continue preaching, but thought of a small experiment to see if her visions would come on command. On March 21, 1619, he summoned Benedetta and told her: "Today is the day of St. Benedict, your saint's day,

go in ecstasy at your pleasure, I give you permission."
That evening, during compline, when the nuns were beginning to chant the *Nunc dimittis*, Benedetta fell into a
trance.[40] Despite the independence afforded her by her
ecstatic voice, her obedience to her superiors was unim-
peachable.

Yet that evening, after Benedetta went to bed, an event
unforeseen by Ricordati took place. Christ again appeared
looking like a handsome young man with long hair and
a long red robe. He was accompanied by St. Catherine of
Siena and other figures of which Benedetta took little
notice since most stayed in the shadows. Her attention
focused on the young man. When she saw him approach,
she turned to Bartolomea, saying: "I don't know if it is
the devil's work; pray to God for me. If it is the devil's
work I will make the sign of the cross on my heart and
he will disappear." The young man explained who he
was and what he came to do: "I have come to take your
heart." She laughed, "What would you do, my Jesus! You
have come to take my heart but I don't want to do it
without permission from my Spiritual Father." He replied,
"Oh, you will see he will have no objections," and reminded her that the confessor had said she could do
anything that was God's will without any reservations.
Convinced by this, and also finding herself powerless to
contravene God's will, Benedetta lay on her back and
asked, "Where will you take my heart from?" "From the
side," he said, whereupon he lifted up his sleeve to mid-
arm and tore her heart from her body. The surge of pain
that went through her almost made her faint, but her
curiosity to see her heart overcame all other feelings and
she asked to see it. It was larger than she had imagined
and still steaming. "No wonder I felt such pain," she
commented. "But how can I live without a heart now that
you have left me without one? How will I be able to love
you?" He replied, "For me, nothing is impossible." Then

he put her heart in his bosom. Benedetta's fear now van-
ished and was replaced with great contentment and a
growing desire to do God's will. Before departing a short
time later, Christ told her to give an account to her confessor of all that had happened.[41]

Benedetta did as she was instructed and lived for three
days, she maintained, without her heart. Her story could
be corroborated by her companion, who was present in
the room when Christ appeared and could hear him speak
through Benedetta, although she could not see him. Bartolomea, moreover, under the pretext of helping Benedetta with her blankets, came up to her and felt her chest
around where her heart should be, and sure enough, she
felt a void.[42] It does not seem, however, that anyone at
this time asked Bartolomea for an account of what she
saw. Benedetta's story appears to have been unchallenged
so there was no need for further evidence. The possibility
of testing Benedetta's or Bartolomea's version of events,
at any rate, ended three days later when Christ returned
to give Benedetta another heart, making it impossible to
verify the incident through a physical examination.

When Christ reappeared, he again came in the middle
of the night with a large retinue of saints. The procession,
preceded by St. Catherine of Siena, seemed festive as it
approached Benedetta's bed. Afraid to look, she lowered
her eyes and asked St. Catherine, "What have all these
people come to do here?" St. Catherine replied, "You will
see." "Why won't you tell me?," said Benedetta. "I want
to know so that I can prepare myself." At that moment,
Jesus approached, holding aloft a heart with three arrows
on top and a gold band around it. "Oh, my bridgegroom,"
exclaimed Benedetta, "did you come to give me back my
heart?" Jesus explained that he wanted her to have his
heart. It was larger than the one he had taken from her,
and the arrows were a sign of the measure of her love
for him; the gold band symbolized her willingness to con-

form to his will. Benedetta opened her arms as if to embrace him, but was so blinded by the splendor of the heart that she could not bring herself to look at it for more than a moment. Jesus then asked her to uncover herself so that he could insert the heart through the same place from which he had taken hers. Benedetta hesitated. "I don't want to disrobe here in the presence of so many people," she said, looking at all the saints that had arranged themselves around her bed. Jesus replied, "where I am, there is no shame," whereupon Benedetta uncovered her left side and he put the heart back in her body.[43] Now the two were united body and soul just like the lovers of a medieval romance.

Whether Benedetta had encountered such tales in her readings, we have no way of knowing. These had, in any event, become part of popular culture and she could well have assimilated them through an oral tradition.[44] Yet the exchange of hearts also had another, more important, source: the lives of the saints. Benedetta had read these as a child and continued to read them along with the other nuns after she joined the Theatines. Since St. Lutgard first united her heart with that of Jesus in the thirteenth century, the exchange of hearts was a prominent feature of the mystical experiences of female saints. Benedetta's favorite saint, Catherine of Siena, lived without her heart for several days in 1370 before she received the purple-red and flaming heart of Christ. And recently, Christ's heart had also been received by Benedetta's near contemporary, St. Catherine Ricci (d. 1590), in the neighboring town of Prato. The notion of the exchange of hearts grew out of two related developments in the devotional practices of female religious: an increased emphasis on the human, male Christ, which enabled them to transform carnal into spiritual love; and increased devotion to the Eucharist, which allowed them to unite both physically and spiritually to the wounds, blood, and heart of Jesus.

The desire for such union was so intense among some female mystics that they had to be restrained from excessively frequent communion. Despite these attempts to curb such demonstrations of piety, however, devotion to the Sacred Heart grew in popularity and received official approval by the Church in the eighteenth century.[45]

Although the exchange of hearts involved pain, the stress of the experience was less on expiation through suffering than on the affective, erotic union with Jesus, the bridegroom. Indeed, Benedetta's pains subsided after she received the stigmata and the dominant imagery in her mystical experiences was that of love, not suffering. "I have given you love," said Jesus, "now return my love." And she did. She felt, in her own words, "in love with Jesus."[46] Her new heart was so filled with love for Him that that she could hardly contain it. Her happiness was indescribable.

But, as in all love affairs, the perfection of the loved one does not always measure up to the expectations of the lover. Despite the praises he heaped on Benedetta during her sermons, Jesus seemed concerned about her purity. Now that she had his heart, he had to protect it from all vice. The vessel in which the heart was incarnate must be worthy of his gift. To maintain Benedetta's physical purity, Jesus ordered her not to eat meat, eggs, and milk products and not to drink anything but water. To maintain her spiritual purity, he assigned her a guardian angel, Splenditello, to point out her failings when she did something unworthy of her beloved. Like the other angels that appeared in Benedetta's visions, Splenditello was a beautiful boy. He was dressed in a white robe with gold embroidered sleeves and wore a gold chain around his neck. His handsome face was framed by long, curly hair crowned by a wreath of flowers. In his hand he held a green wand, about two feet long, on one side of which were flowers, and on the other thorns. The flowers were for when she did things that were pleasing to Jesus, the thorns were to punish her when she did not: "And when I do something wrong, he touches me with the thorny side and makes me feel pain."[47]

If the exchange of hearts and the language of love it engendered signified God's acceptance of Benedetta's feminine brand of spirituality, the dietary prohibitions and the punishments meted out by Splenditello represented a rejection. To be sure, fasting was a regular feature of the ascetic practices of many saints over the centuries, and, like illness, it was a form of renunciation particularly common among women in late medieval and early modern Europe.[48] But whereas for many female mystics, fasting represented a fuller acceptance of their physicality, a way of becoming one with Christ by imitating his *human* suffering, for Benedetta it had very different meaning. Her fasting was not a self-imposed penance, but was rather a divine commandment, something imposed from outside herself to purify her body. Indeed, occasionally she tried to eat some of the forbidden foods, but she choked and vomited what she ate. Instead of being a positive act of penitence, mystical union, and physical self-control, Benedetta's rejection of food was a troubled and negative act. Her fasting reflected a deeply seated ambivalence toward the physical aspects of her feminine self.[49] By fasting she not only rejected the whole realm of food preparation and consumption traditionally associated with women, but she cleansed her body of the impurities of the female sex. For it had been observed by physicians and theologians that fasting curtailed menstruation, one of the curses of Eve. The cleansing effects of fasting paralleled the cleansing effects of washing, which she did with uncommon frequency, to the utter amazement of the other nuns, who had never seen so much washing of the body and such

aversion to dirt.[50] Jesus' commandment that she purify
her physical self implied that if her body followed its own
inclinations it was not acceptable to the bridegroom.

This ambivalence was expressed as well in the angel
Splenditello, who disciplined her by caressing her body
with flowers or scourging it with thorns. Splenditello has
no precedent in either hagiographical literature or iconography. St. Catherine of Siena had seen Jesus holding a
crown of gold in his right hand and a crown of thorns in
his left. But these had referred to his own roles in the
story of redemption and they were not intended for her
discipline. The blossoming wand also appears in her life
as it does in that of St. Fortunatus and St. Christopher,
both of whom were sometimes shown with these in hand.
Yet in none of these instances did the wands contain
thorns. They were not instruments of correction but symbols of the miraculous blossoming of the faith. Most probably, Benedetta's vision of Splenditello grew out of the
devotion to the rosary, with its emphasis on the joys and
the sorrows of the Virgin, which were increasingly de-
picted as flowers and thorns in sixteenth- and seventeenth-century paintings of the Madonna of the Rosary.[51]
That this was the likely source for Splenditello is reinforced by Benedetta's mention that it was while reciting
the rosary that she was struck with the thorny side of the
wand for having misbehaved.[52] Splenditello thus com-
bines elements from a variety of religious images that
helped Benedetta express her troubled relationship both
to Jesus and to herself. On the one hand she was so loved
by him and her own love so pleased him that she was
united with him in a physical and spiritual union that
was reserved for a select few. On the other, she feared
that her very love was not sufficient and her virtues not
pure enough to be acceptable—and the blows from Splenditello's wand confirmed this.

Yet despite these difficulties in love's path, the bonds

between Jesus and Benedetta soon led to marriage. The day after Pentecost (May 20, 1619) Jesus appeared to her in a vision and announced that he wanted to marry her in a solemn ceremony to take place a week later, on the day of the Holy Trinity. He issued detailed instructions on the decorations for the chapel:

> I would like for you to arrange great decorations, so that the upper part of the altar is covered with light blue cloth, the right side with red cloth, and the other two sides in green. The floor should be covered; then let there be 33 lights, a cross with my image on it, an image of the Madonna with the Child in arms, flowers of all sorts and colors, and 12 pillows of various sorts. You will arrange all this according to the inspiration I will give you. . . . And you will put 3 chairs in the choir, facing the altar, then you will call all the nuns in the house and you will begin a procession; you will carry the crucifix ahead of all the others, giving each a lighted candle. And when you will start the procession you will not know where to go or what to say because I will be speaking for you and will explain through your lips the meaning of all these things. Dress two of the novices as angels . . . and place them in the middle of the procession. I would like Father Paolo [Ricordati], Father Antonio Pagni, and Messer Pirro [Torrigiani] to be present and hear all that goes on.[53]

Benedetta hesitated to tell Father Ricordati all the details of her vision. She wondered about the public nature of the event and the work it required. Jesus did not usually reveal himself in such a public fashion. Was this the work of the devil? If so, she wanted nothing to do with it. But if this was a truly extraordinary event arranged by God, was she worthy? There was also something else to consider. She had a feeling that no matter what she did, the marriage was going to take place as Jesus wanted. Yet she doubted that Father Ricordati would give his consent to such elaborate preparations. She would then be put in the awkward position of disobeying her superior, which she had never done before. Torn by these conflicting thoughts, Benedetta did not relate the details of her vision to Father Ricordati until three days later, when, contrary to her expectations, he let her proceed, instructing her to tell the other nuns in the convent so that they could help.[54]

Benedetta did as she was told, but apparently her disclosure was superfluous. The nuns had already started to decorate the convent, something which confirmed her feeling that regardless of her own actions, God's will would be done. She may not have been aware that in one of her ecstasies a day or so before, she had spoken of the impending marriage and the preparations to be made for it and that ever since, the nuns had immersed themselves in a flurry of activity.[55] They sent a servant off to borrow the altar cloths from several people outside the convent. They asked some of the religious institutions in the vicinity to contribute candles, and solicited the pillows and flowers from various other quarters. Naturally, word of what was happening spread and everyone wanted to be in on it, although no one, not even Father Ricordati, was allowed by the provost to enter the convent during the preparations or the ceremony itself. Outside participation was limited to gift giving, which was done with such generosity that the nuns did not know what to do with all the contributions. Many people gave cloths to decorate the walls and the altar. The candles, beautifully large and thick, were sent by the Fathers of the Holy Annunciation and by the convent of Santa Maria Nuova, as well as by people in the mountain country; baskets of flowers arrived from everywhere. The three chairs needed for the ceremony came from the Prior of Pescia. The nuns covered the floor with tapestries, hung the walls and the altar with the cloths, and put flowers around the chapel. Before they could rest from their labors, the day to which they had all looked forward arrived.[56]

On the morning of Holy Trinity, when Benedetta rose
to pray before going into the choir, she heard an inner
voice telling her that she personally should dress the two
novices as angels.[57] She quickly wrote a note to Father
Ricordati to obtain his permission. This done, she and the
others went to the Choir, where she picked up a basket
of flowers, scattered its contents throughout and then lit
the candles, giving one to each. She instructed the nuns
to get on their knees, to remain in the order in which she
placed them and to do exactly as she instructed. Taking
up the crucifix, she began to intone the *Veni Creator Spiritus* as she led a procession out of the choir, on to the
garden, and then back around the choir, where all of them
sang various hymns and the litanies to the Virgin. After
scattering incense and bowing several times in the direction of the altar, Benedetta knelt and resumed her singing
by herself. Some of those present thought she sang in
Latin but the words could not be made out because her
voice was scarcely audible. Quietly, she remained thus
for a short while, gradually losing sight of her surroundings. A great and splendid light then made itself visible
to her and Jesus came forth, so beautiful she could hardly
look at him. Next came the Madonna with a retinue of
angels and saints. Jesus turned to her and said, "*Ecce
ancilla Dei.* (Behold the handmaid of the Lord.) Rejoice,
today I will marry you." Although in her heart she knew
he was Jesus, Benedetta still tried to convince herself otherwise, and replied that she did not want to consent, as
she was not sure whether he was Jesus or the devil. "I
am not the devil, but your Jesus," he answered, "give
me your hand because I want to put the ring on you."
Hearing this, she could not help believing with all her
might, but still she protested, "But Jesus, I am not worthy." The Madonna then took her right hand and Jesus
placed the ring on her finger as she responded, echoing
the words of the Virgin: "Be it unto me according to thy

word." At that moment she experienced such great happiness, such joy, that words could not express her feelings. She felt firm in her desire to do God's will and could
not help loving him and all his creatures. Benedetta kissed
the ring and thanked Jesus for the benefits he conferred
on her. Jesus then told her that no one else would see
the ring but she. He counselled her to be patient in everything for love of him, to take care of the purity of her
heart, and to set a good example for all so that they might
save their souls. The Madonna also admonished her to
guard her heart with great vigilance and to obey her superiors.

Speaking through Benedetta in a tone that seemed to
the other nuns more beautiful than Benedetta's usual voice,
the voice of Jesus then said: "I would like my bride to sit
in that chair in the middle of those three and I would like
to explain, oh sinners, all her virtues from the time of her
birth until now." Benedetta obeyed; the voice continued:
"And so that you, sinners, know that in this, my bride,
there cannot enter the slightest trace of pride or vanity,
it is not she who sees, who speaks, or who hears,
but it is I who see, speak, and work these things in
her."

Jesus went on to recount the story of Benedetta's life,
elaborating on the supernatural events that had taken
place in her childhood and youth: her miraculous birth,
the appearance of the nightingale, the fall of the statue
of the Madonna, and so on. Then he came to more recent
events.

The comet that I recently caused to appear in the sky above
this community signifies the excellence of my bride and
the pain that I made her suffer. . . . If you thought that it
signalled the death of princes, lords, and kings of the world,
it didn't; rather, it meant that the wonders and prodigies
that I work in my bride should be known throughout the
world, since I do them not just for her but for the salvation

of all souls. . . . Now I send you this my servant, who is the greatest that I have in the world, so that you may see that I do not like to dwell in proud hearts that are full of vice . . . but woe to you if you do not make use of her. Oh, my people, I have placed you in her hands and I told her that when she wants me to punish you, she should pray to me and I will punish you immediately, so be sure not to provoke her or me to anger.

Jesus then dwelt at length on the virtues of his handmaid:

If you would know, oh sinner, that even I who am God, was astonished when I saw my bride in the middle of Hell, between fire and iron and with all the demons of the air and Hell coming to torment her . . . and I always found her like a strong column amidst the waves, like gold in the furnace; she was not a false substance made by an alchemist, but pure gold; and again I want to test her and to test her obedience to her superiors and to the prelates . . . because I want you sinners to know that she is not a column of iron or of marble, but of diamonds. I have wanted the signs of my passion to be greater in her today than ever, that my bride have open wounds on her hands and head as I had when I was on the Cross, but not in order that she feel pain, but so that she may feel happiness. I want all who live in this convent to discover these signs so that they may be a constant source of strength and a reminder of my Passion. . . . It was I who ordered that she be the abbess of this convent and I have made her a mirror for all the other nuns. . . . I would like that this, my bride, be empress of all the nuns and I would like that all who dwell in this convent be a constant stimulus to the laity and to all other religious, because I have commanded that they not only be good, but perfectly good, and to those who will not be, I will either send a Devil to tempt them so that in desperation they will leave the convent, or I will send them death because I want all those who live here to be perfectly good.

Jesus concluded by explaining the symbolism of the decorations, some of which were related to the qualities found in Benedetta, and others to the qualities found in himself, the Apostles, and the Virgin. The color green on the altar cloth referred to the hope Benedetta had in him, red to her love of him, and blue to her heart, which always turned to God; the flowers were symbols of all her virtues and the white ones of her purity. The 12 pillows on the other hand, referred to the virtues of the 12 Apostles, the 33 candles to his years on this earth, the three largest to his years of preaching, and the two bands around the largest candle to his charity and that of his mother. Speaking of charity, he mentioned that he was very pleased with the charity of the grand duke of Tuscany who, in that year of scarcity, distributed grain to the poor. He added, "And I want the grand duke to know all these things about my bride, who always prays to me for his wellbeing. . . . And he who does not believe in my bride, shall not be saved."

At the end of this sermon, Benedetta expressed her happiness and gratitude to the Lord by singing the *Te Deum* and *O Glorious Mother*. She then returned to her normal senses and began to leave the choir, almost as if nothing had happened. Along the way she stopped to chat about other matters with the wife of the Vicar who, in defiance of the provost's orders, had come to the convent to witness the wedding.

Benedetta's nonchalance, however, was not shared by the other participants in the event. Something significant *had* happened. Or, they began to wonder, had it? No one other than Benedetta had seen Jesus, the Madonna, the saints, or the ring. And this raised greater doubts and concerns than Benedetta's previous mystical experiences. Everyone knew that St. Catherine's marriage had left no visible signs, yet there was something or perhaps a number of things that were different and troubling about Benedetta's marriage, which taken together could no longer be ignored. The very call for a semi-public ceremony implied that witnesses would see some supernatural persons or objects, yet these had not appeared. Then there was the request that notable people, the grand duke no less, be notified of Benedetta's deeds. The desire for publicity was unusual for a true mystic. Contemporaries were well aware that because women were denied a place in the social and public discourse of their age, they sought to make their voices heard in other ways. Many a female visionary was in reality a woman seeking attention and power. Still fresh in people's minds were memories of the infamous Maria de la Visitación, the nun from Lisbon, who by virtue of the stigmata and of visionary powers became one of the most influential European women of the 1580s, consulted by rulers and high church officials, before she was discovered to be a fraud.[58] Could Benedetta's case be similar? If so, it would be better to find out now. As the wedding preparations had already demonstrated, despite the provost's feeble efforts to curb any publicity about the affair, many people had become interested in Benedetta's mystical powers. If the numbers kept on growing and involved highly placed individuals, the affair might get out of hand and it would be difficult for the ecclesiastical authorities to control. The sudden sense of urgency about the case may also have been strengthened by Jesus' extravagant words of praise for Benedetta and the threat of damnation for those who did not believe in her. Such behavior was not characteristic of holy people, whose messages from the divine contained praises of the Lord rather than themselves and who gained followers by their character and deportment rather than by threats. Yet if the threats were believed by the simple and untutored, it would be much more difficult to discredit them later on. Speaking through Benedetta, Jesus had said that the fate of the townspeople was in her hands.

The greater the number of people who believed that, the harder it would be to curb her influence if she turned out to be a fake. There was nothing to be gained from delay. The provost of Pescia ordered all those who had witnessed the events of the day to talk no further about them with outsiders. Benedetta was relieved of her duties as abbess until further notice. The investigation began the next day.

CHAPTER FOUR

The First Investigation

THE PROVOST OF PESCIA, Stefano Cecchi, who was the leading ecclesiastical official in the town, came to examine Benedetta himself. He was accompanied by several of his subordinates and a scribe to take notes. The provost was an elderly but vigorous man, a member of one of the richest and most powerful families of Pescia. He was used to taking charge. Indeed, this is how he had become provost nearly twenty years earlier. For when in 1600 Pope Clement VIII nominated a Florentine nobleman, Bernardo Segni, to the post, it did not occur to Cecchi to sit idly by and watch the dignity of the office, not to say the living to be made from it, slip from the grasp of his family, which had shared it with the Turini family for almost a century. His vigorous protests blocked the appointment of Segni and led to his own appointment instead. Once in power, he continued to pursue his course with equal vitality. For two decades he actively campaigned to make Pescia a bishopric, with himself, naturally, as its first incumbent, while at the same time he manged to preside with a firm hand over the ecclesiastical affairs of a rapidly changing jurisdiction. Cecchi, in short, was not a man who would relish being either deceived or ignored.[1] He

would look into the happenings at the convent of the
Theatines with a great deal of care. At stake was not only
the status of the convent but his own reputation and the
continuing campaign to raise Pescia to a higher ecclesiastical dignity.

The first order of business was to examine the stigmata,
since they were the only visible signs of miraculous intervention. Christ had said during Benedetta's sermon of
the previous day that the wounds on her body would be
open and larger in appearance than before. The provost
therefore looked at her hands, feet, and side, where he
could see bits of dried blood about the size of a small
coin. When they were washed with warm water, each
revealed a small opening from which drops of fresh blood
trickled out. When the blood was dried with a towel, more
came out. Similarly, on Benedetta's head there were a
large number of bloody marks, which also bled into the
towel when washed with warm water. The stigmata, which
up to the day before had been nothing more than small
red marks on Benedetta's body, had changed just as Christ
predicted.

After the physical examination, the provost asked Benedetta to recount for him how those wounds came to be
on her body. She then told how Jesus had appeared during Lent and through rays that came forth from his body
had imprinted his wounds on her during the middle of
the night. "How many rays did you see?" the provost
asked. "Five big ones, but there were rather more that
came from the head, though small ones," she replied.
"How did you arrange your feet while you were lying in
bed so that one was on top of the other?" She answered,
"I did not put them one on top of the other, but I found
them well arranged, one on top of the other, without
their hurting me in this position." The provost then asked,
"Do you have continuous pain in those signs?" "On Sundays," she replied, "they seem to be numb; on Mondays

and Tuesdays I have almost no pain; and all the other days I have great pain, especially on Fridays."[2] With this, the first visit ended.

The provost and his retinue returned for a second look ten days later (7 June, 1619). Benedetta, in the meantime, had written to Paolo Ricordati about her most recent vision and had also requested a meeting with the provost. As in his first visit, Cecchi began by examining the stigmata. He could see the same signs as before but noted a few changes. The wound on the right hand did not bleed when washed and dried with a towel. The puncture marks on the head were also dried and looked partly healed. He then asked Benedetta what she wanted to tell him, but she seemed nonplussed and had nothing to say. True, she had written a letter to her confessor describing a vision. That letter was written in the same handwriting as the letter the provost now showed her. But she could not recall having written anything about wanting a meeting with him. The provost was perplexed, but there was nothing to be done and the visit came to an end.[3]

The puzzle was not resolved until the ninth visit, which took place the following month. Benedetta revealed that on the day prior to the above visit, Jesus in the form of the crucified and bleeding Christ, had made himself visible to her in a vision and told her he "wanted to influence the opinions her superiors had about her."[4] She was to obtain permission from her confessor to write the provost. Jesus would tell her what to write, just as he would tell her what to say when the provost would come to see her.[5] "You will tell him on my behalf, that I have elected this convent for myself, and that I want him to take special care of it, because I want all those who live in it to think that they are in a special place dedicated to me, with a greater obligation than other nuns to strive for perfection."[6] Because she was in a trance when she wrote the letter to Ricordati, she did not recall all of its details afterward, but remembered only that she had asked for permission to write directly to Stefano Cecchi—a request Ricordati denied on the grounds that if Christ really wanted to communicate with the provost, he would find other means for doing so. As it turned out, both Benedetta and the confessor got their way, as Ricordati forwarded to the provost the letter that Benedetta had written to himself. Yet when the provost came the next day, Jesus was less intent on molding his opinion than on testing him. Instead of speaking through Benedetta, as he had originally intended, he remained silent to see if the provost believed in her,[7] but he did not tell Benedetta what he had done or his purpose for doing so until the end of June, hence Benedetta's inexplicable silence during the interview earlier that month.

By way of contrast, the next examination, on June 14, provided dramatic evidence of Christ's continuing interest in making his presence known through the person of Benedetta. The usual observation of the stigmata revealed that some of the wounds that had almost healed the week before were now bleeding again and when the provost ordered Benedetta's hair cut and washed so as to make the wounds more visible, the punctures on her head appeared to have fresh blood on them. At this point Benedetta was allowed to leave the room briefly to rearrange and close her garments, before returning for further questioning. The proceedings, however, were interrupted abruptly when she ran back in, holding her hands to her head. "Jesus, what is this?" she exclaimed, as blood gushed down her face and on to the floor. The visitors quickly got some towels and managed to stanch the bood but the examination had to be cut short because Benedetta was in too much pain to continue.[8] Yet this was not the end of the investigation, just a postponement. The questions in the minds of the ecclesiastical authorities were not dispelled by a bit of blood.

If such a positive demonstration of divine power was not sufficient to convert doubters into believers, perhaps fear of divine wrath would accomplish the same end. While the visits of the authorities continued during the month of June, Benedetta revealed to Father Ricordati that she had again seen Jesus in a vision. This time he was an angry and vengeful Christ, a Christ sitting in majesty, surrounded by his celestial court, his sword unsheathed, ready to strike. His anger was directed at the people of Pescia. There was no one there, he said, who was willing to ask for his mercy, of which they were much in need because of the gravity of their sins. He would punish them with the plague to make them see the folly of their ways. Benedetta offered to pray for his mercy herself and to be the instrument of the town's salvation by spending her time in purgatory until the day of judgment. Christ's anger seemed to be appeased by her words. He told her to continue to love him always and to arrange for processions to placate him. This she did, for no sooner did she tell Ricordati what she had seen, than he gave her permission to organize a procession with an image of Christ at the head.[9] The threat of plague was not to be taken lightly. Pescia had been spared the dread disease for a long time, but the danger was never far removed. The Pesciatines knew from their own past experience, as well as that of their neighbors, that as much as a quarter or even a third of the population could be snuffed out in a matter of weeks. Moreover, Pescia had not yet fully recovered from the grain shortage that had overtaken the whole state that year, and it was common knowledge that famines and epidemics went hand in hand.[10] In light of all this, it was only prudent to follow Benedetta's advice and, if not yet to embrace her as the instrument of Pesciatine salvation, at least not to reject her claims out of hand.

The investigation thus advanced carefully and cautiously. Between late May, when it started, and early September, when the first round ended, there was a total of fourteen visits, all of them recorded by a scribe. What transpired during these meetings can be reconstructed only in part. Some of the original transcripts do not survive, and the questions asked by the provost were only occasionally written down. Yet by interpolating the line of inquiry into the structure of the testimony, it is possible to recreate much of the investigation.[11] In addition, fuller accounts of similar cases can supplement the remaining material. For in the previous centuries a great many investigations of mystical claims had taken place and much had been written on what to do in such situations. Cases of fraudulent sanctity were commonly heard by Church tribunals. Ecclesiastical officials like Stefano Cecchi, who needed help in determining the validity of the cases that came before them, could consult any number of manuals that were compiled for that purpose.[12]

What then were the questions asked of Benedetta and what do they imply about the criteria for judging the merits of her case? The most obvious place to start was with the miraculous signs since they were the only evidence that could be verified by the senses. For this reason the first four sessions dealt exclusively with the stigmata. First came the physical examinations of the wounds to ascertain that they were genuine and not painted on. Then came detailed questions about how the miracle occurred. The examiners wanted to know exactly how the wounds were imprinted in Benedetta's body. Did they just appear or were they produced by the rays emanating from Christ? If the latter, how many were there? These were not idle inquiries, but were designed to elicit a clear picture of what went on and to determine if Benedetta's account held up to the rules governing the physical world. The question about the number of rays, for instance, produced the answer that there were five rays, and not six, as could well have been the case since there were six wounded areas: four in the limbs, one on the side of the rib cage, and one on the head. This then meant that Benedetta must have had her feet crossed one on top of the other, so that only one ray was needed to pierce both. But, as the provost's next question intimated, to cross one's feet in this manner, while lying down is extremely difficult. How did Benedetta do it? Her reply, that her body was arranged in this position without her knowing how, meant that this part of her story did not conform to the usual behavior observed in the natural world.[13]

Interest in the stigmata continued throughout the ecclesiastical investigation, but after the fourth visit the provost began to explore other areas as well. Was Benedetta certain that she had experienced visions? Perhaps she had simply imagined them from the readings and prayers that had preceded them; perhaps they were dreams. To determine this, he asked her about the circumstances surrounding her visions. How long ago did they start? What was she doing at the onset of each? How long did each vision last? Benedetta's answers suggested that she had not been dreaming. Most of her visions occurred in the midst of her daily activities rather than in bed, and, indeed, what was happening around her at the onset and at the end of her visions allowed her to make a rough estimate of how long they lasted.

Having eliminated the possibility that they might be dreams, Cecchi still needed to ascertain whether what Benedetta experienced were the vain imaginings of an overly enthusiastic nun. Many theologians and religious thinkers had written about this problem, St. Teresa being one of the most recent: "If anyone tries to pass beyond this [the first] stage of prayer and lift up his spirit so as to experience consolations which are not being given to him, I think he is losing both in the one respect and in the other. . . . It seems to be a kind of pride that makes

us wish to rise higher. . . . It is specially harmful for
women to make such attempts, because the devil can
foster illusions in them."[14]

Had Benedetta encouraged her visions or had she tried
to repress them? The search for mystical experiences was
inimical to humility, the most fundamental characteristic
of a true seer. This notion informs many of the questions
posed by Stefano Cecchi. When the angel came to take
her to the Mount of Perfection, did Benedetta attempt to
stay behind? Did she resist when the Virgin announced
that she would give her a guardian angel? Did she try
not to see Splenditello whenever he appeared in front of
her? Had she considered the possibility that the marks
on her body were the work of the devil and not of God?[15]

Benedetta's answers to these questions reveal her efforts
to remain within theologically acceptable boundaries. Before ascending the Mount of Perfection, she "strained to
remain in herself and at prayer like the other nuns and
as part of that effort she made the sign of the cross. And
when she made the sign, she departed from her normal
senses . . . When she heard the Madonna say she wanted
to give her an angel . . . she couldn't help but believe
her, even though she tried not to, and . . . she tried
violently, many times, not to believe in the visions." She
tested Splenditello to determine whether he came from
God or from the devil by telling him "that he should pay
homage to the name of Jesus while she said the name out
loud. And when she did this three times, she saw that
as soon as she said the name the first time, he bowed
down with his head almost to the ground." Yet it occurred
to her afterward that even this test might be inconclusive
"because the Devil could do that to make me believe, but
then a certain hope grew in me that I was not deluded,
but not even because of this did I think that bowing to
the name of God was the work of God." Her attempts to
deny her mystical experiences went even further: "She

has the certainty in herself that the signs on her hands, head, feet, and side are the work of God, but she has not consented to them, and it is against her will. And the other morning, while she was doing silk work, this certainty came to her mind and she did not want it, and she said to herself, this is not the work of God but of the Devil, and to lift the certainty from her mind she went to wash her hands in the hot water of the silk reeling basin to disdain the Devil. She thought she would die of pain but nonetheless her belief remained."[16]

Benedetta thus argued that she found herself constrained to believe despite the efforts of her will. Yet she was careful not to make unwarranted claims and to distinguish between certainty and belief. She admitted that none of her tests gave her absolute certainty and talked in terms of belief rather than thought, of hope rather than incontrovertible proof. Her hope grew out of the strength of her belief, which overcame all her rational efforts. These distinctions conformed to the pronouncements of theologians, who acknowledged that there were no infallible tests for discerning true visions from diabolical illusions. All they could offer were guidelines for recognizing the characteristics most likely to be present in a genuine vision and those that were incongruent with divine revelation.[17]

Beyond the problem of differentiating between dreams, illusions, and true visions, Benedetta's examiners also wanted to know the exact kind of vision she may have experienced. This was difficult to do since, as St. Teresa and others acknowledged, the "interior things of the spirit are so hard to describe, and still more so in such a way as to be understood."[18] In the thirteenth century, St. Thomas Aquinas had distinguished between visions and ecstasies, and within each category discussed the variety of ways in which the mind apprehended divine truth, i.e., through the senses, the imagination, and the intellect.[19] These categories corresponded roughly to the mystical states described four hundred years later by St. Teresa, who differentiated between the union of the soul and rapture and who, like St. Thomas, apprehended three varieties of divine locutions.[20] In the state of mystical union, according to St. Teresa, "the soul becomes conscious that it is fainting almost completely away. . . . It gradually ceases to breathe and all its bodily strength begins to fail it: it cannot even move its hands without great pain; its eyes involuntarily close, or, if they remain open, they can hardly see. . . . He can hear, but he cannot understand what he hears. He can apprehend nothing with the senses . . . in this condition all outward strength vanishes, while the strength of the soul increases so that it may the better have fruition of its bliss."[21] In this state, it is still possible to resist God, and to prevent the union. This is not the case with rapture, which is a more sudden and violent flight of the spirit, and is so intense that no resistance is possible. In rapture, the soul "can still hear and understand, but only dimly, as though from a long way off." At its highest point, however, "it can neither see, nor hear, nor perceive." And afterward, "if the rapture has been deep, the faculties may remain absorbed for a day or two . . . and be as if in a state of stupor, so that they seem to be no longer themselves."[22]

It is clear from Benedetta's testimony that the questions put to her were informed by these distinctions with regard to mystical states. Her statement that she thought she was not drawn out of her senses and that she was aware of the presence of the other nuns when she had the vision of wild animals was surely a response to a question about her sensory awareness during that experience. Her answer must have allowed Cecchi to determine that her vision involved neither mystical union nor ecstasy. Questions about later visions, however, elicited different responses. When asked about her state of being when she saw the Mount of Perfection, she replied: "She did not think she was in herself like the other times, being unable to see the other sisters nor being aware of what she was doing . . . and when she made the sign [of the cross] she departed from her normal senses."[23] Similarly, when asked about how she arrived at the vision of the enclosed garden, she answered that "when she was abstracted from her senses, she felt violently drawn. No one led her to the garden, but she suddenly found herself there."[24] Benedetta's diminished awareness of her surroundings and her inability to resist the pull of the visions were indicative of a state of ecstasy. In this condition, did she communicate with God through the senses, the imagination, or the intellect? "Did you actually *hear* a voice when you were led up the Mount of Perfection?" she must have been asked. "I heard the voice of the boy as I hear the voice of your Reverence when you examine me." Did she actually *see* St. Peter in one of her visions? "She saw St. Peter in person and not in her imagination."[25] Did she see the young men who beat her? "She saw them infallibly, as she sees your Reverence." Did she see Jesus and the Virgin during the mystical marriage? "She saw them infallibly and not in her imagination." Her ecstasies, then, seemed real but they were of a lesser kind than those of the imagination or the intellect, which according to St. Thomas were more perfect manifestations of divine truth than those perceived through the senses because they needed fewer aids to be apprehended and understood.[26]

In addition to their concern about the type of visions she experienced, Benedetta's examiners queried her about the orthodoxy of what she saw and heard. Divinely inspired visions, according to Church theologians, did not promote doctrines or practices that were contrary to the teachings of the Church.[27] It is for this reason, for example, that Cecchi showed a great deal of interest in Benedetta's vision of the enclosed garden, which she described in early July and to which he returned for clari-

fication a month later. What was the meaning of the flowers, and the lights, and the gold spout in the fountain?,
he asked. Benedetta answered all of his queries, "the
flowers were the virtues whose scent please God . . . the
lights signify that whoever has virtue, gives virtue to others, because virtue always lights the way . . . the gold
pipe stands for my father confessor, who guides me to
perfection and to the fountain of God's grace, without
whom it would not be possible to receive the spout, or
the water, or the grace of God." The purpose of Cecchi's
questions was to see if Benedetta thought she could receive God's grace without the help of her superiors. If
the water in the fountain represented salvation, could
Benedetta quench her thirst without the aid of the Holy
Catholic Church? Her answers must have laid to rest any
fears he may have had about her beliefs. It was clear from
her interpretation of this and other visions that she never
questioned the need for obedience to the ecclesiastical
authorities.[28]

Related concerns about orthodoxy also led the provost
to ask about a vision in which St. Peter, dressed in priestly
robes, said Mass and gave Benedetta communion. The
right to administer the sacraments was strictly limited to
the priesthood and was one of the most powerful instruments in the hands of the ecclesiastical authorities. In the
previous millennia the Church had battled a variety of
heretical sects that advocated different views on the subject. Had Benedetta ever heard anyone say that the sacraments could be administered to the faithful directly by
the saints? Did she believe that the presence of a priest
was not necessary to receive the sacraments? Was there,
moreover, anything in the way the Mass was conducted
that did not conform to orthodox practices? What did St.
Peter use for the host? Did his prayers differ from the
usual ones recited by Catholic priests? Although the fact
of the vision remained troubling because of its implication

that someone outside the ecclesiastical hierarchy could give communion, Benedetta's testimony was reassuring with respect to the use of sacred objects and the correct form of prayer: "The holy sacrament and the host seemed to her to be just like the ordinary ones when she communicates; and the priest [St. Peter] said the customary words when he gave her communion."[29]

Another form of heretical thought common among mystics was the belief that through prayer and divine union they might transcend the shackles of personal sin. Their own state of perfection, in turn, could serve others as a direct channel for grace. Stefano Cecchi scrutinized Benedetta's testimony for traces of this line of thought, focusing particularly on her account of Jesus' admonition "that she should take care of the purity of her heart and give a good example to all the nuns so that they might save themselves."[30] In his visit of 15 July, which was primarily devoted to clarifying the testimony of the previous session, he carefully came back to this statement. Did Benedetta believe that she was capable of a greater degree of perfection than other people? Did she believe that she could guarantee the salvation of others? ". . . she always believed without doubt that all she could do, the others could do as well," she replied. "And she meant to be a good example to all those with whom she talked. She is not sure that all who would follow her example would be saved, but only hopes so, having always placed her hope in God."[31]

Having satisfied themselves that the content and meaning of her visions were not contrary to the Faith, the authorities also made certain to examine the effect of the visions once Benedetta returned to normal. Genuine visions, it was believed, did not make the visionary proud of the favors received from God. Instead, they gave rise to greater humility and the realization that the gifts bestowed on the soul were not the result of its own merits but a free gift of God. In grateful response, the soul of a true visionary felt a renewed ardor to pursue the path of virtue and to share with others the spiritual benefits received. In contrast, arrogance and lack of charity after seeing apparitions pointed to demonic illusions.[32] The testimony elicited from Benedetta was meant to clarify this point. Explaining the feelings she had after the vision of the enclosed garden, she said that "she had a greater desire to be good than before." And after receiving the heart of Christ, she "felt greater desire to do God's will . . . and calling Jesus and talking with the other nuns about the love of God she feels her desire for God's love grow."[33] Similarly, when Jesus placed the ring on her finger, she "felt such joy and contentment that she could not help but love God and mankind . . . and when told to do certain things for the love of God and mankind and for the sake of obedience, she seems to feel the same interior happiness that she felt the day she received the ring and she always feels a desire for the salvation of all."[34]

Yet despite these claims to feelings of charity and love toward others, several statements in Benedetta's testimony pointed to tensions with those around her. Early on, during the fifth visit to the convent, when Benedetta had talked about the wand that her angel used to discipline her, she inadvertently revealed more about her relationships with the other nuns than she may have intended. As an example of Splenditello's use of the wand, she recalled that he once hit her hand with the thorny side "after I hit a young girl on the back because her shouts made it impossible to hear the rosary, which was being recited in a low voice."[35] Another hint that something might be amiss came from Benedetta's remarks a month later, when she discussed how Jesus wanted the provost to help make the convent a place of special virtue. Her statement summarizing Christ's instructions implicitly criticized the behavior of the nuns. The provost "should make sure that they remain secluded and well enclosed and that there be an end to the talking with lay people at the doors and at the grate . . . and when they must talk with men, they should always have two companions with them so that the Devil not put harmful thoughts in their heads."[36] It also seems clear that at least some of the nuns who bore the brunt of Benedetta's criticisms did not take kindly to her behavior. Benedetta complained to Father Ricordati about how some of them were not treating her very well.[37]

That such behavior between cloistered and secular people might have taken place is not surprising given the social function of convents in the seventeenth century. Neither is it difficult to believe that tensions could arise among the nuns about this and many other issues. Convents brought together women of real religious vocation with those who had none. They required that women of widely disparate levels of wealth, education, and age interact every day in close proximity to each other, under rigid rules of behavior, and all this with virtually no possibility of leaving. When nuns entered a convent they brought with them well-developed notions of family solidarity, political factionalism, and economic standing, which were at odds with the institutional rules of obedience and humility. Inevitably, power struggles, alliances, and, occasionally, violence ensued. In mid-sixteenth century, for example, Sister Cassandra Capponi escaped from a nearby convent in Fucecchio and refused to return because she feared she might be killed by some of the nuns who were her enemies. Several years earlier, at the same convent, Sister Giulia della Luna had stabbed a nine-year-old convent girl to death with a pair of scissors, and another young novice was treated so cruelly at the hands of Sister Caterina de' Brunaccini that in desperation she threw herself in the convent's well and drowned.[38]

These occurrences were, of course, extraordinary. Murder was not an everyday event in Tuscan convents. But like the famous case of the nun of Monza, which in the early seventeenth century resulted in the death of two convent women, these extraordinary situations reminded officials of the dangers inherent in the internal dynamics of convent life.[39] For these cases, though unusual, were part of a continuum in which commonly exchanged insults, outbursts of rage, and slaps sometimes escalated to more serious levels of violence. Indeed, both religious and secular authorities in the sixteenth and seventeenth centuries spent much of their time trying to contain the petty squabbles that were the common stuff of contemporary convent life. They feared such situations might erupt into more dangerous conflicts that would spill over into factional quarrels outside the convent walls.[40] Thus, the blow Benedetta gave another nun, the criticisms she leveled at her companions, and the words of self-praise she uttered as Jesus during her mystical marriage, while a far cry from the murders committed at Monza and Fucecchio, pointed to a dangerous kind of righteous arrogance that would need to be explored.

The ecclesiastical authorities decided to question some of the other nuns in the convent. On July 23, their tenth visit, they met with the new abbess, Felice di Giovanni Guerrini, with Bartolomea Crivelli, who was Benedetta's companion, and with another nun, Margherita d'Iptolito Ricordati, a relative of the convent's father confessor. Judging from the statements made by the three women, the questions they were asked centered on Benedetta's mystical marriage. This was the most obvious event with which to begin, since it had precipitated the investigation and had included verbal threats against skeptical bystanders. The event was also witnessed by all three nuns and their recollections of what happened would clarify much of what Benedetta herself had said about it.

The testimonies offered by the three witnesses, it turned out, did not result in any major new revelations. They merely confirmed what the authorities had heard before— that Benedetta had made unusual claims, that speaking as Jesus she had been full of praise for her own virtues, and that she had threatened those who did not believe her with eternal damnation. The usefulness of the three accounts, then, lay not so much in their novelty, but in the fact that they reinforced each other and that they did so with a remarkable attention to detail. Almost every aspect of the wedding preparations and of the ceremony itself was vividly recalled—a tribute to the memories of the nuns and to the importance attached to ritual in seventeenth-century life. Despite one nun's apologies for not remembering everything because Benedetta "said so many things that I get confused,"⁴¹ few modern observers would recall so well the details of a ceremony that lasted for more than three hours.

At the conclusion of each of the statements the nuns were asked if they had obeyed their orders not to talk with anyone outside the convent about the mystical marriage. As one would expect, all answered they had remained silent. But Felice Guerrini's testimony contains an interesting addition: "One evening, when she [Benedetta] was in ecstasy, she can't recall whether it was Wednesday or Friday, she heard her say, 'why do these ingrates not want my treasure to be discovered? I will make it known to other people on the outside and I will make them come from far away.' "⁴² This boldly stated desire for publicity was stronger than any made previously and suggested that Jesus, speaking through Benedetta, was growing increasingly impatient with the pace of the proceedings and the cloak of silence the investigators wanted to maintain.⁴³ On the other hand, Benedetta herself had expressed dismay at the spread of her notoriety. She testified that she was upset when a young nun came to tell her that news of her mystical experiences had spread to the outside. "And this was against her wishes because she did not want anyone to talk with her about it."[44] Similarly, she did not express any regret when asked about how she felt about the fact that the provost had not allowed Paolo Ricordati, Antonio Pagni, or Pirro Torrigiani to attend the wedding. After telling herself that everything should be done according to the rules of obedience, she did not think about it any further. And when asked whether she had asked the wife of the last vicar to be present at the ceremony, she replied that she didn't know who had done so, although she conceded that she may have told her something about it when she saw her the day before.[45]

Yet, if the major obstacle to officially sanctioned public recognition was the absence of a ring to attest to a mystical marriage, there need have been no further delay. At the end of her testimony, the last witness, Margherita Ricordati, mentioned almost as an aside, that the day before she had seen a ring on Benedetta's finger. She "was unable to see it well because [Benedetta] always covers up that hand," but she had seen enough of it to tell the examiners that it had a "yellow band with a cross . . . and it doesn't look so much like a ring but a yellow mark with a cross."[46]

Needless to say, this announcement must have caused quite a stir and Benedetta was called in to the examination room. There, on the fourth finger of her right hand, plain for everyone to see, was "a circle, the width of an ordinary, inexpensive gold ring . . . and on the top side there were five points, four of which are the size of ordinary pin heads, and in the middle, there is another like the point of a pin of an almost dark red color."[47] Miraculously, the sign that everyone wanted to see had appeared.

The ecclesiastical examiners were eager to probe further but Benedetta, after a brief appearance, was feeling too ill to answer. The visit was forced to a close and the

questions postponed for future meetings. When the officials returned, a week later (1 August, 1619), they added
an inspection of the ring to the usual examination of the
stigmata. This would remain the standard procedure until
their last visit on September 9. As for how the ring got
there, Benedetta explained that its appearance did not
involve any further miraculous interventions of which she
was aware. The ring looked to her as it had always looked
since her marriage to Christ. If there was a change it was
only in the perception of others who could now see something that was there all along.[48]

It was to others, then, that the investigators turned
during the next meeting. Having gathered an eyewitness
account of the mystical marriage, they now wanted similar
reports of other events. They questioned two nuns, Felice
Guerrini and Sister Angelina, about the comet that had
appeared earlier that year. Disturbances of nature—an
unusually violent storm, the emergence of a bright new
star—these and other signs often presaged the coming of
a holy person. Both nuns answered that they had seen
the comet. Felice stated that she had seen it for several
days and that the nuns were told by people on the outside
that it was located over the convent.[49]

The authorities also wanted to know what happened
on the day of the Holy Spirit (20 May, 1619), when Felice
and Angelina, with the help of other nuns, decorated the
refectory with flowers and placed a statue of the baby
Jesus on a pillow in the hopes that the Holy Spirit would
partake of the meal. Asked if either one had seen the
Holy Spirit that day, they both answered that they had
not and that no one else had seen it either, but, clearly,
expectations were running high that Benedetta would.
Indeed, Felice and Angelina had called her into the room
after they decorated it, to get her approval and Benedetta
not only approved but wanted the baby Jesus placed in
a spot where she could easily see him. So confident were

the nuns in Benedetta's mystical gifts that the seat next
to hers became a coveted place of honor, which Felice
declined because she did not want the adulation of the
other nuns. Her hopes and those of the others were not
totally dashed. Although they themselves did not see the
Holy Spirit, when Benedetta gazed on the figure of the
infant Jesus, she saw the dove of the Holy Spirit suddenly
descend on the assembled group. Her trance lasted several hours.[50]

The final witness to appear before the group was Bartolomea Crivelli, Benedetta's companion for the last two
years. She would provide information about events not
seen by anyone else. Bartolomea testified that she had
shared a room with Benedetta for several years and told
of the help she provided during those long, pain-filled
nights, when Benedetta would ask her to put her hand
on her heart so as to alleviate her suffering. Her job was
not easy: "While I had my hand there," she commented,
"it felt as if a dagger were hitting it. . . . and with my
hand in place she seemed to flail around less but when
I didn't have my hand there, she could not stay in bed
because of the great pain she experienced. And I would
work so hard that I would sweat. . . . and one could
smell an awful sulphorous stink coming out of her mouth.
. . . Sometimes she would call me twice a night . . . and
she would say, 'Hold me, help me.' . . . as soon as I
heard her, I would put my hand on her heart and I would
quiet her."[51] Asked if Benedetta ever told her the cause
of her pain, Bartolomea replied, "She never told me what
caused it, but when I would say that Jesus wanted to test
her, she would confirm it." Asked if she ever saw anyone
appear, Bartolomea answered, "I never saw anyone, but
I heard her talk and say that she did not want to leave
this place but would rather be ill for the love of Jesus."
Bartolomea then corroborated Benedetta's account of how
Jesus took her heart. From her vantage point on the other

side of the curtain that surrounded the bed, she could see Benedetta and overhear her conversation. But she was careful to move away as soon as Benedetta began to emerge from her trance, for fear of being criticized if seen.

Bartolomea recounted further how she had been present three days later, when Jesus returned to give Benedetta his heart. Again she watched from behind the curtain after Benedetta dismissed her for the evening. "I didn't want to leave," she said, "and indeed I couldn't leave, feeling as if I were being held there." She heard St. Catherine and then Jesus speak to Benedetta, and saw her uncover the side of her torso, which disclosed a mark that was larger and redder than before. "And when He put [the heart] inside her I began to see that the flesh rose up and moved slowly, slowly with those rays in front; and all the ribs . . . were lifted up. And when it arrived at the place where the heart belongs, it stopped . . . and the heart reentered its place. But it was so large that one could see it would never fit and it raised her flesh. Then she covered herself up again, but before she did that, I touched it [the heart] and it felt very large and so hot that my hand could not stand it." Shortly afterward, Benedetta began to come out of her trance and Bartolomea retired to her own bed on the other side of the room. Asked by the examiners if she had been afraid during any of the above, she replied: "When I was there, I did not have any fear but rather contentment. Neither did I fear when she was assailed and had those pains." Asked if she had ever seen any apparitions, she answered she had not. And in response to a query about whether she had actually seen Benedetta's heart or that of Jesus, she again answered she had not.

The final event described by Bartolomea was the placement of the stigmata. Her account was identical to Benedetta's so not much new was learned. Again she was asked if she had seen anyone and she answered she had not. She merely overheard the conversation between Benedetta and Jesus and saw the marks on her body. Before she concluded her testimony, Bartolomea was enjoined not to talk with anyone about what she had seen or heard. With this, the interrogation of witnesses other than Benedetta ended. Monsignor Cecchi and his colleagues returned three more times during the next month to examine the stigmata and the ring as well as to clarify a few points that still seemed unclear. Benedetta was shown the transcripts of all previous visits and was asked to verify that the information they contained was accurate.[52]

After two months of extensive questions and fourteen visits to the convent, the investigation, as far as the participants were concerned, had ended. What did the authorities accomplish? In addition to scrupulous examinations of the stigmata, which enabled them to ascertain their legitimacy, Cecchi and his colleagues were able to learn a great deal about the quality and content of Benedetta's mystical experiences as well as about her character and deportment. Her visions seemed genuine; they were neither dreams nor fantasies, and their religious content conformed to church dogma and practice. Many of them could be corroborated by witnesses who not only saw her fall into trances, but who heard the voices of divine apparitions issue from her mouth. One witness, Bartolomea Crivelli, had also been present when she received the stigmata and Christ's heart and could support Benedetta's claims from visual evidence. She saw marks on Benedetta's body that had not been there before and she saw the moving bulge of Christ's heart as it was put in place. In addition, Benedetta's attitude was appropriate for a divinely inspired visionary. She was reticent toward her mystical experiences and she repeatedly expressed a continued desire to obey her superiors and to shun publicity. This suggested that she was not given to pride, the devil's gateway. In short, if the criteria for judging a true visionary were the presence of verifiable signs, the orthodoxy of the visions, and the character and comportment of the visionary, then Benedetta seemed to fill all the requirements.

On the other hand, no investigation is without its problems or unresolved questions, and this was no exception. The voices that spoke through Benedetta during her trances heaped such praise on her virtues that they seemed incompatible with a holy person. Books of saints' lives showed that their visions included praises for the Lord and other holy figures, not for themselves. In contrast, the words that issued from Benedetta's mouth sounded vain and immodest: "And that which she said about her birth and about Benedetta and in praise of her is suspected of having been said to induce her to vainglory."[53]

Similarly, Benedetta's zeal in reprimanding the other nuns in the convent for failing to live up to her standards may have indicated that she had an exaggerated sense of her own good qualities and that she easily gave way to anger. St. Teresa and others had warned of the dangers of such zeal for those who were just beginning to walk on the road to perfection. The misdirected concern for the behavior of others rather than oneself was a trap set by the devil to ensnare the unwary.[54]

Finally, there was the claim that the fate of the Pesciatine people was in Benedetta's hands, that she could determine whether they would be severely punished or saved. This kind of statement might be a deliberate effort to coerce the community. By means of this threat she might simply arrogate as much power to herself as possible.

Yet, in her defense, it could be argued that it was not Benedetta, but Jesus, that spoke the words in her praise. How could she be held accountable for statements that were not her own? Hadn't Jesus himself said: "And so that you, sinners, know that in this, my bride, there cannot enter the slightest trace of pride or vanity, it is not

she who sees, who speaks, or who hears, but it is I."[55]
Indeed, when she was not in a trance and she discussed
with her examiners whether she thought she was free
from sin, she made no extraordinary claims to perfection,
not even as a recollection of words said to her by Jesus
during her visions. It is only from the statements of the
others that the authorities learned of the esteem in which
Jesus held her. In her own testimony she made no mention of Jesus' praise and stressed her sense of her own
unworthiness to receive spiritual gifts.

As for her zeal in trying to discipline others, one had
to remember that after all she had been the abbess of the
convent. She was responsible for the spiritual welfare of
all the nuns. If she did not discipline them, who would?
And perhaps she was justified in her actions. Nuns should
not be talking and shouting during the recitation of the
rosary or carrying on with laypeople at the gate.

Finally, her claim that the fate of other people depended
on her and that she could successfully intercede with Jesus
on their behalf may not have been extravagant. Visionaries had long served as protectors of the devout and as
mediators with God. Just a few years before, for example,
the Venerable Ursula (1547–1618), the foundress of the
order of Theatine nuns, had reported that God had appeared to her in a vision and said that he would inflict
terrible punishments on the city of Naples unless the
inhabitants did as she said.[56] Thanks to her intercession
Naples was spared and from then on she was seen as the
city's protectress. Visionaries told ordinary people what
Christ wanted from them and helped guide them toward
salvation. Like Christ, they also could help to save others
because their own personal sacrifices, achieved through
a lifetime of ascetic denial, made their prayers particularly
pleasing to God. For Benedetta's contemporaries, then,
her statements were not necessarily a calculated ploy for
power and influence but could be legitimate messages

from God and sincere efforts to intercede for humanity.[57]

In short, there seemed to be plausible explanations for the most troublesome questions in Benedetta's case. Cecchi and his associates therefore departed, confident that they had explored every question thoroughly and that Benedetta appeared to be a true visionary. When the convent was granted full enclosure in July of the following year, Benedetta was reinstated as abbess.

CHAPTER FIVE

─────────────────◈◈◈─────────────────

The Second Investigation

IF BENEDETTA'S REINSTATEMENT to her post as abbess can be seen as a return to normalcy, then the scant documentation for subsequent years tends to confirm it. In the eyes of Benedetta's contemporaries, nothing sufficiently noteworthy to merit written mention occurred in the Theatine convent. Yet this is precisely what is most remarkable. For, during a period of over two years, Benedetta led a double life—as administrator and spiritual leader of a convent on the one hand, and as mystic on the other—and managed to fulfill both roles adequately enough to satisfy local officials and the nuns under her charge.

This was a notable achievement, since it took considerable talent to be a good abbess. Because she was responsible for the temporal as well as the spiritual welfare of her convent, an abbess' duties led in two very different directions—the material world and the world of the spirit. Her responsibilities included the appointment of nuns to the customary offices of a convent—portress, treasurer, mistress of the novices, and so on—which had to be filled with capable women: the treasurer should be literate and familiar with bookkeeping; the mistress of the novices should be a good teacher; the cook should know how to plan the purchase, storage, and preparation of food as well as how to supervise the kitchen staff.[1]

In addition, the abbess was concerned with the financial standing of the convent and its economic and political relations with the outside world. This entailed making sure that the rents on the convent's properties were collected, that the tenants maintained the land and all agricultural capital in it, and that contracts were fulfilled. It also meant she had to supervise the nuns' manual labor, especially the reeling of silk, which contributed to the convent's income, and she had to tap potential sources of funds from charitable bequests or from the dowries of new entrants.

Since the nuns were cloistered, a board of outside administrators aided Benedetta with some of these tasks. Members of the board helped to manage the convent's properties and market its silk and agricultural products. They also helped to raise funds from donors and acted as financial mediators with outsiders. Because the board's composition was crucial to the welfare of the convent, much care was taken in its selection. In the fall of 1620, we find Benedetta participating in the appointment of board members with a sharp eye to maximizing the benefits to the Theatines. At the request of the vicar and the provost of Pescia she submitted the names of eight possible candidates, but sent along a letter arguing in favor of her four favorites—Lorenzo Pagni, Oratio Forti, Pirro Torrigiani, and Francesco Berindelli—all mature and wealthy men who, she pointed out, were past benefactors of the convent. It did not require much reading between the lines to surmise from her letter that she hoped the four would continue to channel some of their considerable wealth to the Theatines.[2]

With regard to the spiritual welfare of her convent, Benedetta's duties were no less demanding. Abbesses were supposed to be spiritual guides to the nuns under them. They saw to it that the daily religious observances of their convents were kept and that the nuns conducted themselves with modesty, humility, and love toward one another. They were responsible in great measure for the inner progress of each of the nuns under their care. Although they did not supplant the convent's father confessor, they worked in close association with him and were supposed to lead exemplary lives that the other nuns might imitate.[3]

Charged with these varied tasks, the life of an abbess was solidly anchored in the social and spiritual needs of her convent. Yet amid these responsibilities, Benedetta kept up her role as mediator with the world of the supernatural. During the first two years of the Theatines' enclosure her visions continued on a regular basis. Some of these simply elaborated earlier themes, especially that of the convent's need to maintain the proper observance of religious rituals. But, gradually, there surfaced a new concern, undoubtedly related to the death of Benedetta's father sometime between November 1620 and March 1621. Giuliano's demise not only reminded her of her own mortality, but must have left her with a profound sense of loss. There was no one left in whose heart she held the special place that she had held in his. As a result, in 1621, while Benedetta went into her trances, one of her guardian angels, Tesauriello Fiorito, began to prophesy her imminent death. He would urge the nuns to treat their abbess with greater tenderness than before because her days on earth were numbered. Only after her death would they realize her true value. They knew full well, he reminded them, that there was no one else in the convent as fit to be their abbess as she. Emerging from her visions Benedetta herself began to speak about her death and even had her grave opened and readied for the day when it would be needed.[4]

She did not have to wait long. On the day of the Annunciation, 1621, the Theatine nuns witnessed Benedetta's death. The agitated sisters quickly called Paolo Ricordati, their confessor, to see what he could do. The well-meaning Father arrived immediately and commanded Benedetta in a loud voice to return to the living, which, to everyone's astonishment, had the desired effect. When Benedetta revived, she told the assembled what she had seen on the other side. Accompanied by Tesauriello, her soul passed from this life to the next, where demons battled for its possession. But the angel Gabriel, armed with some holy oil from the church of Santa Maria of Pescia, came to the rescue and delivered her soul to Purgatory. Its stay there was brief—just long enough to say a Hail Mary and to pray for the release of the other souls, including that of her recently deceased father. Her prayer was granted. Thus she found herself in Paradise in the presence of the Heavenly Host, surrounded by the souls of her loved ones. Her happiness was so great, she recounted, that when she heard Father Ricordati calling out to her in a voice that boomed through Paradise, she did not want to leave. Only God's command and his reassurance that she would come back persuaded her to return to life. Before she departed God also told her that eventually Father Ricordati and the Provost of Pescia would be there as well, as would the nuns of the convent if they behaved as they should.[5]

The nuns must have interpreted these cautionary words with mixed emotions. They were undoubtedly delighted that their visionary was still with them. After all, it was precisely in order to keep her in their midst that they called Father Ricordati. Benedetta's mystical powers could be of enormous benefit to the convent and each of the nuns in it, as her account of her death once more reminded them. Her casual mention of the power of the holy oil from the provostial church, for example, would

surely please Monsignor Cecchi, who would quickly perceive the usefulness of her statement for his attempts to
have the church become a cathedral. In his pleasure, he
might reward the convent with an additional source of
income. On a more spiritual plane, the story of Benedetta's death would have reminded the nuns that she could
intercede with God on their behalf. Her prayers could
mean the difference between painful years in Purgatory
and a blissful journey to Paradise.

But their gladness was certainly tinged with resentment
and no small element of fear. If she could help them get
to Paradise, she could just as easily send them in the
other direction. Moreover, the nuns had begun to chafe
at her frequent admonitions about the inadequacies of
their behavior. Tesauriello's warning to the nuns that no
one else would be as competent an abbess as Benedetta
was surely a response to increasingly open hostility to
her rule. Some of the nuns may have begun to talk openly
about electing another abbess when Benedetta's customary three-year term was up.[6] It was useful to have someone like Benedetta in the convent, but it was also desirable
to curb her power, if so doing did not imperil the state
of one's soul or the prestige of the convent.

This careful balance was difficult to achieve. And the
Theatines ultimately failed. What happened next is not
easy to decipher from the scattered records that survive.
Whether the nuns tried to elect someone else but could
not get Benedetta's cooperation, whether a routine bureaucratic examination of his jurisdiction brought the
Theatines to the attention of a newly appointed papal
nuncio in Florence, whether negotiations for a merger
between the Pesciatine Fathers of the Holy Annunciation
and the order of the Barnabites brought some sceptical
minds to the scene, or whether another convent, jealous
of competition, once more raised the issue of Benedetta's
legitimacy as a visionary, we shall probably never know.

What we can ascertain is that sometime between August 1622 and March 1623, the papal nuncio, who as the representative of the Holy See had jurisdiction over the provostrie of Pescia, sent several of his officials to investigate Benedetta's claims. The results of this investigation, which they sent to the nuncio, Alfonso Giglioli, in the form of a "Brief discourse," must have intensified that prelate's worst fears.[7]

Perhaps this is not too surprising. The nuncio's emissaries, having less at stake than previous investigators, undoubtedly embarked on their mission with a more skeptical attitude. Unlike the Theatine nuns, or Father Ricordati, or Monsignor Cecchi, they had nothing to gain from Benedetta's claims. If she was a visionary, she was just one more in a long line of Catholic seers; she would not add much to the greatness of the Church. If, on the other hand, she was not a visionary, there was much prestige and credibility to be lost by letting her continue. The Church had already seen too many impostors and deceivers in the previous half century to want to encourage any more. Indeed, perhaps in reaction to the excessive displays of religious fervor among certain mystics or possibly in response to the jibes of Protestant critics, the Church from the sixteenth century on had actively discouraged popular belief in unauthenticated visions and miracles. This attitude is evident in the premise with which the nuncio's men began their report: "all novelty is dangerous and all unusual events (*singolarità*) are suspect." The angel of darkness often transformed himself into the angel of light to deceive the simple. Therefore, as "those who were well versed" in the ways of God, and as Benedetta herself had apparently agreed, "it was probable that though she was a good servant of God, she was deluded by the Devil." The doubts of the investigators about the reported miracles and visions were strengthened by their interpretation of Benedetta's character. They

did not find in her "that true and real spiritual foundation
which God's grace presupposes." Neither did they see
"the charity, humility, patience, obedience, modesty . . .
or other virtues to that eminent and heroic degree with
which they usually accompany the true spirit of God."[8]
These were the qualities that the reformed Church of
Benedetta's time was beginning to stress in its leading
figures. Rather than reward miracle workers and inter-
cessors with the supernatural world, who might be nothing more than magicians, the ecclesiastical authorities recognized the sanctity of individuals whose exemplary lives
others might follow and whose evangelical work strengthened the power and influence of the Church. The can-
onizations of Charles Borromeo, Ignatius Loyola, and Philip
Neri in the early seventeenth century were part of this
redefined conception of sanctity. Benedetta's path to holiness was based on a different and somewhat outdated
model, that of miracle worker and intercessor for ordinary
mortals. She lacked the extraordinary personal virtues that
would make her a role model for other good Christians.
Moreover, the content of her message did not promote
the cause of God or his Church.

Because God's purpose was to strengthen belief in himself and his representatives on earth, according to the
nunzio's emissaries, he never did anything that was alien
to his goodness or did not reflect the splendor of his
majesty. Yet there was much in the supernatural events
the examiners heard or read about, as well as in Benedetta's behavior, that seemed contrary to these guidelines.
Her visions, for instance, contained contradictions, although it was obvious to all that God neither lied nor was
ever contrary to himself. Benedetta claimed, for example,
that in one of her visions the Virgin had asked her to
obtain permission from Father Ricordati to have a guardian angel but, prior to this request, such an angel had
already appeared in her early visions.

Her mystical experiences also contained immodest and lascivious language, which "God dislikes." Benedetta's initial reluctance to uncover herself in the presence of Christ and his reply that where he was there was no shame, "partook more of the lascivious than of the divine."

Her visions, moreover, turned her away from the path of true religion. "They were not a result of prayer, but impediments to it, since they occurred at the start rather than during the fervor of prayer." And some of them, such as the one of St. Peter offering her communion, if not manifest errors, were at least suspect. As for the stigmata, which unlike the visions were visible to all, they were obviously not the marks of Christ but of the devil "because everyone knows that this can happen only during the fervor of prayer, in the harshness of the desert, or during periods of solitude," and not while lying softly in bed where the enemy of God resides. In fact, just prior to receiving the stigmata, "the devil had appeared in front of her as a beautiful young man to seduce her, which makes it probable that he suddenly changed himself into the form of Christ to deceive her under the pretext of goodness, since he had been unable to do it through evil."

The report was also critical of the mystical marriage. It was, above all, a great display of vanity. Benedetta's lengthy ecstatic praise of her own virtues during the ceremony and her allusions to being sanctified were sacrilegious. If Christ had been the bridegroom, he would not have called for such a public show or elaborate preparations. He was himself the carrier of all glory and splendor and therefore delighted in working secretly. But, if he had ordered a public wedding, his only purpose could have been to let the witnesses see the signs of the miracle, and none were seen until two months later, when a rather shabby looking ring, not nearly as beautiful and brilliant as the one Benedetta had described, appeared on her right hand. Christ also would not have allowed opposition to his plans to alter the wedding preparations he had ordered. Yet, although he had requested the presence of Father Ricordati, Father Antonio Pagni, and Pirro Torrigiani, none of them had been allowed to attend.

Because Jesus was all-powerful, further doubt was cast on the divinity of Benedetta's mystical experiences by the kind of assistance he seemed to need from ordinary mortals. On receiving her new heart, for example, she had needed the help of her companion, Bartolomea, to keep it in place. Jesus' heart was so much larger than her own that it kept protruding from her chest until Bartolomea pressed down on it. The investigators found it hard to believe that Jesus would need such help to finish his miracles. For the same reason, they found the shields, wands, and other devices used by Benedetta's angels superfluous. Common angels were powerful enough to accomplish their tasks without extra equipment.

In addition, there were other worries about the angels. Benedetta had begun to claim that not only she but all the Theatine fathers were guarded by two angels each. Such assertions, according to the investigators, cast the seeds for the spread of false doctrines and should be denied. Her so-called angels, moreover, bore peculiar names—Splenditello, Tesauriello Fiorito, Virtudioello, Radicello. These sounded more like the names of bad spirits than of heavenly creatures.[9]

In conclusion, the report noted that matters had gone too far and that in part Father Ricordati had been responsible for allowing the situation to get out of hand. The poor father, now seventy-five years old, was "a good and simple man." But "he had been and still is too ready to believe without proof or experience." His credulity "has given the devil a free rein to keep deluding this poor creature."[10]

To bolster their contention that she was not a true visionary, the investigators then added that there was no lack of people of high standing at Pescia who thought that "Benedetta was obsessed or vexed by the devil."[11] And here, they availed themselves of the age old distrust of the people of the plains for those of the mountains, a distrust rooted in the violent tenor and poverty of mountain life, and coupled it to the notion that communing with the devil was hereditary. People suddenly remembered that her father and mother had also been possessed, "as had and still are many people of her homeland and of those surrounding areas." The devil, as was well known, liked those high, isolated places, where Roman Catholicism had gained only a precarious foothold, and where magic and superstition abounded.[12] Mountain people had long been considered by those of the plains to be ignorant and dull-witted, hardly fit to be included in the company of other men. In their squalor and ignorance, they often turned for support to the devil rather than Christ and, having fallen into his clutches, they found that they and their offspring were inextricably bound to his malevolent designs.[13] Thus, despite the fact that Benedetta had spent more than twenty years in the plains, the taint of the mountains still clung to her.

In the minds of the investigators, the most obvious link between Benedetta's demonic obsession and that of her forebears was her attitude toward food. Ostensibly, she had been unable to eat meat or milk products. She had even vomited when her superiors, in order to test her willingness to obey, ordered her to eat the foods that Christ had forbidden her. Yet despite this seeming aversion, she concealed a desire for salami and Cremonese style mortadella, which came to light when she was seen secretly fetching these items to where she could eat them undisturbed. This craving was "similar to her father's

when he too was assailed by spirits," and a strong indication that the daughter had inherited her family's demonic obsession.

In view of these grave doubts and accusations regarding
Benedetta's claims, the ecclesiastical officials who wrote
the report recommended that a more thorough investigation be undertaken. Its purpose would be to discover
once and for all the nature of the spirits that assailed her.
Until the conclusion of such an investigation, their findings would remain "within the realm of the probable,"
rather than "within the realm of certain truth." Their
request, they said, was urgent because they feared for the
spiritual safety of the convent, "in which there were many
young girls of great good will." To protect them from
harm, they wrote to the nunzio, would be "an act of great
charity."

The nunzio agreed. After reading the report, he sent
the investigators back to Pescia with new instructions.
Since they had already questioned Benedetta once and
had looked at all the materials from the provost's earlier
investigation, they were to expand their inquiry by closely
questioning all the other nuns in the convent. If necessary,
they were also to reexamine Benedetta.[14]

The officials did as they were told, wishing, undoubtedly, to bring the affair to an end as quickly and conclu-
sively as possible. Two trips to Pescia must have been
quite enough for clerics interested in larger problems than
those of a small-town nun who may have strayed from
the true path. Perhaps this is why they presented their
findings in the most resolute way possible. Whereas in
the previous report, they had couched their statements
in the language of probability, there was no room for
doubt in the second. They had found the absolute truth:
"It is certain," they wrote, "that Benedetta's visions and
ecstasies are demonic illusions."[15] But because the precise
nature of these illusions and the deeds to which they gave

rise were much worse than anything they or others might have imagined, they also wanted to make sure that "everyone may see on what this truth is based." The investigators therefore wrote down in great detail "what the nuns said about this affair," carefully indicating next to each charge just how many nuns had come forth with supporting testimony. All of their conclusions were thus based on the observations of others as well as their own.

Previously, the sole indications of the probable demonic origins of Benedetta's visions had been the contradictions in her statements and her eating of certain foods in secret. Now their report contained additional evidence. For example, one nun discredited Benedetta's claim, made when she spoke as an angel in one of her ecstasies, that the Theatines could learn from her how to flagellate themselves with true spiritual fervor. The nun, who had been standing nearby, noticed that Benedetta did not strike herself even once, and that to make it seem as though she had, she smeared the whip with blood from the wounds in her hands.

Another nun had seen her put her own blood on a statue of Christ, which Benedetta then claimed began to bleed in honor of her own sanctity. The nun told the investigators that she had immediately informed Father Ricordati, but nothing came of it because of the way he handled it: Ricordati ordered her to disclose what she had seen to all the other nuns when they met together in the refectory. But when she began to do so, Benedetta fell into a trance and, speaking as St. Paul, admonished her with such a terrible voice, that she became terror stricken and unable to continue. Benedetta then forced her to discipline herself with her whip in the presence of the others.

Further damaging testimony about Benedetta's visions came from another nun who, along with the rest of the convent, had heard an angel say through Benedetta that she was so pleasing to Christ that he once descended from a crucifix and tenderly kissed her forehead, leaving behind a gold star that would soon be visible to all. The star did indeed appear on Benedetta's forehead not long thereafter. But the nun told the investigators that Benedetta had made the star herself with some gold foil and had fixed it in place with red wax. The nun had found this out by peeking through a hole in the door of Benedetta's study.

Citing this and other evidence, the ecclesiastical officials concluded: "Here is the vanity and falsity of her ecstasies; it would be impossible to finish telling them all, suffice it only by way of conclusion to this chapter [of the report] that both the Angels and God, or to put it better, those pretending in ecstasy that they were the Angels and God, spoke words of love and shameless words and they went to great efforts to persuade one nun in particular that it was not a sin to engage in the most immodest acts."

Before getting to those aspects of the case, however, the officials went on to analyze the stigmata. "Beyond what was said in the previous report, we add that from what we have heard from the nuns, there can be no doubt, indeed, it is held as certain, that they are the work of the devil." The basis for this statement was the testimony of two nuns who spied on Benedetta through the hole in the study door. More than twenty times they saw her renewing her wounds with a large needle. Other nuns had similar stories. Three observed that her wounds varied in size, and that sometimes, after she locked herself in her study, she would emerge a short while later with freshly bleeding wounds. One nun who usually washed her hair testified that "she has seen her locked in her study in front of a mirror, taking blood from her wound with a large needle and putting it on her head." Three nuns also reported that she sometimes ran barefoot through the convent as if her feet were healed. And one heard her exclaim as she jumped down from a small table,

"Whoever saw me jump down would say that there's nothing wrong with my feet."

Benedetta's mystical marriage turned out to be equally false. Many of the nuns had become suspicious of the ring, the alleged proof of the marriage, ever since they noticed that the adjoining fingers were sometimes stained with the same shade of yellow as the ring. Some had also noticed that the ring changed in appearance, sometimes being very bright and at other times faded. Now Benedetta's companion, Bartolomea, came forward with strong evidence that the ring was not genuine. She told the investigators that Benedetta's own mother, who occasionally came to visit her daughter in the convent, had been "very troubled and afflicted" by the thought that the ring might not be real. When one day she confided her fears to Bartolomea, the latter afterward took it upon herself to search through Benedetta's desk, where she eventually found a small brass box containing diluted saffron. She surmised that Benedetta used the saffron to paint the ring and that she used her own blood for making the red stones.

As for the exchange of hearts, quite apart from the unseemly words that passed back and forth between Christ and Benedetta, "which partake more of the lascivious than of the divine," the investigators noted with impeccable logic, that "if there had been a real change of her heart into that of Almighty God, there would have been as a consequence a union of God and her superiors, who represent that self-same God, and . . . one can see that the contrary has happened." In short, since the investigators represented the Church, and the Church represented God, if Benedetta's heart were really divine, then she and the investigators would be in agreement about the nature of the supernatural events that had taken place at the convent.

Bit by bit, the ecclesiastical authorities chipped away at

the miracles that had allegedly occurred through Sister Benedetta. They dealt with each and every one of her visions, arguing from Scripture or other sources against the logic and probability of such visions; they found evidence that the stigmata, first those of the feet, then of the hand, and finally those around her head, were self-inflicted. They also found witnesses who testified against the genuineness of her ring and the authenticity of her alleged "death."

Why was it that now the ecclesiastical authorities were suddenly able to find so much evidence against Benedetta? Why was it that so many of the nuns were willing to speak up against her? Why, for that matter, had they kept silent for so long? Benedetta's success in passing herself off as a mystic and recipient of divine favors had required a long conspiracy of silence. It had been four years since she first received the stigmata and the ring; two years since she was resurrected from the dead. If the nuns had seen her repeatedly inflicting her own wounds, if they had seen her fashion her own ring, and felt her pulse under her sleeve when she lay as if dead, why did they wait until now to make their charges?

Many in the convent had probably believed Benedetta at first. Had not her own companion, Sister Bartolomea, witnessed the imprinting of the stigmata? Moreover, everyone could see the blood and the ring with their own eyes. In the beginning the nuns may have wanted to believe. Theirs was a new religious house; a house influenced by the zeal of sixteenth-century Catholic reform. Perhaps God wanted to single them out to point the way to a revitalized Church.

If any of them had begun to suspect that something was amiss at this time, they probably kept silent because a scandal would surely damage their efforts to obtain enclosure. It might also hurt them financially by turning away from the convent the parents of prospective entrants as well as potential donors.

But it may well be, of course, that it was not until later that suspicions began to grow. Possibly Benedetta became increasingly careless about her deceptions once she felt securely settled in her role as abbess of a regularly established convent.[16] If this was so, then the nuns would have had no strong evidence against her until after they received full enclosure in the summer of 1620. Still, that leaves unexplained why no one said anything until three years later.

The nuns' long delay in bringing their accusations to the authorities was not just a matter of self-interest on their part, even if this may have been the original reason for their silence. In subsequent years their actions were governed to a large extent by fear—fear of Benedetta, fear of their confessor, fear of the provost. That Benedetta could be a formidable person to cross is not difficult to believe. Some of the nuns told the nuncio's emissaries that even though she claimed to be perfect, she was in reality haughty and easily bore a grudge. She was also cunning, claiming, for instance, that her imperfections were a disguise to camouflage the dazzling brightness of her virtue. And she was not above using violence to get her way, as several incidents had revealed. What would happen if they disclosed what they had seen to Father Ricordati? One nun had already tried, with rather disastrous results. By ordering her to tell the whole convent, including Benedetta, what she had told him, he left her unprotected, allowing the abbess to silence and punish her. Her example was undoubtedly a deterrent to anyone else with similar notions. As the report to the nuncio suggested, Ricordati's ineptness in this as in other instances was a crucial factor in allowing the situation to continue as long as it did. Although in earlier years the confessor may have tried to keep an open mind with regard to Benedetta's claims, he was indeed, "too ready to believe," and by now he had become too much a part of the events that Benedetta directed to see his way clearly through the conflicting accounts that were made of her miracles. He had, after all, even raised her from the dead.

With no help coming from Father Ricordati, it must have been difficult for those who wanted to expose Benedetta to know where to turn next. Surely not to the provost, Monsignor Cecchi, who had already investigated Benedetta's claims and had judged them valid. Better to remain silent until some other opportunity opened up. The right moment came along in 1623, shortly after Alfonso Giglioli expressed further interest in Benedetta's case. What created this opportunity was the initiation of efforts by the Fathers of the Holy Annunciation to join the Barnabites, one of the strictest orders to emerge from the Catholic reform movement. The stern Barnabites were likely to view Benedetta's claims with great skepticism and would frown on any notoriety that might cling to the Fathers of the Annunciation because of their relationship to the Theatine nuns. Fear of jeopardizing the delicate talks for a merger must have weakened Father Ricordati's willingness to come to Benedetta's defense. And once the merger took place in September 1623, his ability to aid her was undermined by this rapidly failing health. At age 76, his last reserves of energy had been used up by his negotiations to ensure a safe and stable place for his congregation within a larger order. He died on 18 October, 1623—a month after his work was completed.[17]

With one of Benedetta's supporters ailing and preoccupied with other matters and the other preempted by the authority of the nuncio, Benedetta was left in an extremely vulnerable position. Because the Theatine nuns were an independent congregation, Benedetta had no other ecclesiastical protectors. She could not count on the institutional support that might have been available to her had she been affiliated with a larger order. Moreover, as an outsider in Pesciatine society, she had no secular allies or patrons among the people that mattered in the town. Hadn't "people of high standing" already complained that she was obsessed by the devil, as were her ancestors? Benedetta's lack of support among the ecclesiastic or secular hierarchy probably made all the difference at this point.[18] The nuns at last felt safe to reveal what they had long concealed.

The most damaging testimony the authorities heard, however, did not have to do with the wounds of Christ, or the ring, or the faked death, or the pretensions to living sainthood. Incriminating as all these were, similar discoveries had been made in other cases and such irregularities were to be expected. Much worse than that, and what the nuncio's emissaries had been totally unprepared for, were the revelations made by Sister Bartolomea Crivelli, Benedetta's special companion during the previous years. She was the nun whom Benedetta persuaded to "engage in the most immodest acts," and who now, prodded by a sense of "very great shame," was ready to talk. Though the clerics hinted at her disclosures in the opening of their report, they saved them until last because they would illuminate better than anything else the true nature of the events that took place at the Theatine convent: "But let us come to the deeds worked through Sister Benedetta by the said angels," they wrote, "so that they may clarify whether they are angels of Paradise or demons from Hell."

"This Sister Benedetta, then, for two continuous years, at least three times a week, in the evening after disrobing and going to bed would wait for her companion to disrobe, and pretending to need her, would call. When Bartolomea would come over, Benedetta would grab her by the arm and throw her by force on the bed. Embracing her, she would put her under herself and kissing her as

if she were a man, she would speak words of love to her.
And she would stir on top of her so much that both of
them corrupted themselves. And thus by force she held
her sometimes one, sometimes two, and sometimes three
hours. . . ."

Bartolomea's testimony must have stunned her lis-
teners. Some of them may have read about such cases in
the legal commentaries of Antonio Gomez, Gregorio Lopez, or Prospero Farinacci, which had been printed and
widely circulated throughout Italy in the previous decades. Nonetheless, it was one thing to read about such
things and another to hear about them firsthand. To anyone's knowledge, there had been nothing like it in any
Italian convents.[19] So disturbing was Bartolomea's testimony for the scribe who recorded it that he lost his usual
composure. His handwriting, so neat and orderly up to
now, grew illegible. His words, and even some of his
phrases, had to be crossed out and rewritten. The officials
who heard Bartolomea's story entirely lacked either an
intellectual or an imaginative schema that would incorporate the kind of behavior she described.

The problem was not that sexual misconduct involving
nuns was unknown—the Pesciatine convent of Santa Chiara
during these years was evidence to the contrary—but that
heretofore it always involved male lovers. Church authorities knew what to think about and what to do with
heterosexual behavior among nuns or priests. They also
were well versed in the literature on male homosexuality,
especially in monasteries. These sins were discussed in
almost all the penitentials as well as in the sermons of
popular preachers. Dozens of ecclesiastical and secular
laws and hundreds, if not thousands, of cases tried by
the courts had provided a framework for dealing with
such situations. Yet that two women should seek sexual
gratification with each other was virtually inconceivable.

But the clerics who questioned Bartolomea were, of

course, more interested in her reaction to what had happened than in their scribe's. Did she not think, they must have asked, that she was transgressing against God's commandments? Bartolomea answered that "to entice her and deceive her further, Benedetta would tell her that neither she nor Benedetta were sinning because it was the Angel Splenditello and not she that did these things. And she spoke always with the voice with which Splenditello always spoke through Benedetta. . . ."

As a further inducement to silence, Splenditello held forth the promise that eventually Bartolomea too would see his angelic presence:

> Splenditello asked her many times to pledge that she would always be his beloved and promised that he would be hers, and that after Benedetta's death he would always be with her and she would see him in the same way that Benedetta herself saw him. He persuaded her many times not to confess their mutual doings, telling her that she did not sin. And while she did these indecent things to her, he told her many times: give yourself to me with all your heart and soul and then let me do as I wish, that I will give you as much pleasure as you would want.

Sensing at times that Bartolomea was not fully convinced, Jesus himself would occasionally speak through Benedetta before making love. One time he told Bartolomea that he wanted her for his bride and that she should give him her hand. Another time, when she was in the choir, Jesus held her hands and told her that he forgave her all her past sins. And on another occasion, "after she was distraught by these things, he told her that there was no sin whatsoever and that Benedetta, in doing them, was not aware of them."

Unlike Bartolomea, the ecclesiastical officials who heard her testimony did not believe that the relationship between the two nuns was sinless. But the question was, what sins had they committed? To determine this they had to establish as precisely as possible what the two nuns did with each other. It was clear from Bartolomea's testimony that no "material instruments" were involved in the relationship. But the officials found out that they engaged in other practices, which according to some jurists were equally offensive. In addition to acts of simple lust, such as Benedetta's kissing of Bartolomea's breasts, the two women had engaged in mutual masturbation until they achieved orgasm. On being questioned in detail about their sexual practices, Bartolomea related that Benedetta grabbed her "hand by force, and putting it under herself, she would have her put her finger into her genitals, and holding it there she stirred herself so much that she corrupted herself . . . and also by force she would put her own hand under her companion and her finger into her genitals and corrupted her."

While the above act might be construed as *mollitia*, additional testimony suggested that because the two women engaged in genital rubbing as one lay on top of the other, they may have committed sodomy. According to Bartolomea, Benedetta "would force her on the bed and embracing her would put her under herself . . . and she would stir on top of her so much that both of them corrupted themselves." Such rubbing together of the genitals and the "spilling of seed" assumed to occur during orgasm could be interpreted as the classic form of female sodomy.

Having established what had occurred as clearly as they knew how, the investigators also wanted to know how long these affairs had gone on ("for over two years"), how often ("at least three times a week," "eight to ten times she disrobed," "up to twenty times she kissed her genitals by force"), and under what circumstances: ". . . she not only sinned with her companion during the night, but also many times during the day, when she would pretend to be sick and remain in bed while the other nuns were at their prayers or at work."

One of the discoveries they made was that during daytime hours, Benedetta's study became an even more convenient meeting place than her cell. The abbess' access to the study thus facilitated the illicit encounters between the two nuns. Since Bartolomea was illiterate, Benedetta offered to teach her to read and write, giving the two women an added opportunity to meet unobserved without arousing suspicion. To avoid censure, Benedetta went to obtain permission for the lessons from Father Ricordati, who, like Heloise's uncle in an earlier love story, had no idea that the lessons taught would be of a rather different sort than those he had in mind. In the guise of Splenditello, Benedetta taught her companion to write, but while teaching her, she "would touch her breasts and her neck and kiss her, telling her words of love."

As the ecclesiastical investigators listened to Bartolomea's testimony, what "caused most horror," they said, was the fact that these "shameless deeds" took place "during the most solemn hours of our Lord and of his Mother and other saints," and that "after doing these indecent things they went to take communion without confessing." For the authorities, Bartolomea's and Benedetta's lack of respect for the Holy Sacrament and their casual observance of church rituals was one of the msot troubling aspects of the case. The circumstances in which they carried on their relationship and their disdain for their spiritual obligations were as damning as what they did. It bordered on sacrilege.

Because the deeds performed by the two nuns were viewed by the investigators with such horror, they were eager to determine the extent of Bartolomea's cooperation in the affair. Had she willingly made love with Benedetta or had she tried to resist her advances? In all of her replies, Bartolomea was careful to establish that she was forced into the relationship: "taking her by force . . . by force she threw her on the bed . . . by force she put her hand under her." She also added that several times when Benedetta called her at night she refused to come. The result, however, was that "Benedetta went to find her in her bed and, climbing on top, sinned with her by force." During the day, resistance was easier. She claimed that sometimes, when she anticipated what Benedetta wanted to do, she was more successful getting away. Even so, her ordeal was not always over. If Benedetta could not catch her, "with her own hands she would corrupt herself" in Bartolomea's presence.

If trying to flee from Benedetta did not solve Bartolomea's problem, why did she not tell anyone? Her answer to her examiners was twofold. On the one hand she had been persuaded by Splenditello that she had not sinned; on the other, "she kept silent as much from shame as from the little confidence she had in the father confessor." Here again, Paolo Ricordati's failure to take a more decisive and skeptical stance toward Benedetta seems to have been a crucial element in allowing the situation to continue.

Yet, before accepting Bartolomea's version of the relationship, as the ecclesiastical authorities appear to have done, it would be wise to probe a little further. There may have been considerable truth in her account. Perhaps she did believe that Benedetta transformed herself into an angel from heaven. When Benedetta spoke as Splenditello her voice sounded different from her normal voice and she sometimes spoke in another, presumably heavenly, language. Her appearance also changed, so that according not only to Bartolomea but to other observers as well, she took on the looks of a beautiful young boy of fifteen or sixteen. The society in which Bartolomea lived was a religious society in which the supernatural, the miraculous, actively intruded in everyday life. Bartolomea

was a young, illiterate girl, for whom Splenditello may
have been a very real presence. Apparitions and voices
were a common and accepted means of communication
between ordinary people and the supernatural world. More
cultured and literate people than she believed in them,
including Father Ricordati, a former lawyer trained in
judging evidence, and Monsignor Cecchi, the provost.
Benedetta, moreover, could be very persuasive in all of
her guises. She was bright, she had a rudimentary education, and she was imaginative. She had managed to
convince Bartolomea that she had seen the imprinting of
the stigmata and that she had felt a void in her chest
when Christ removed her heart. She also arranged for
her to feel Christ's larger heart when it was placed in her
body. For Bartolomea then to doubt the reality of Splenditello would have been to question the evidence of her
own senses and the authority of those who were presumably wiser and older than herself. And it may well be that
if she thought it was Splenditello and not Benedetta who
made love to her, she may have felt flattered to be the
object of his attention. She, too, would have been the
recipient of special divine favors. Moreover, if it was
Splenditello and not Benedetta, she had to consider his
warning. He had cautioned her not to confess her sexual
encounters. What would happen if she did? Would some
terrible form of divine retribution strike her for her dis-
obedience?

But if she did believe in Splenditello and kept quiet,
out of a mixture of both joy and fear, why did she feel
shame? There was considerable ambiguity in her statements. For her admission to feeling shame implied that
she was not fully convinced that her relationship was
made in heaven.

If this was so, she may have remained silent because
of fear that Splenditello was a demon. It was common
knowledge that true angels did not lure people into im-

moral acts. Lustful angels were fallen angels, and perhaps Bartolomea was ashamed that she had been so easily seduced by the false promises of the devil.

Yet if Bartolomea's silence was related to her fear of Splenditello, whether angel or demon, why did she not confess after she discovered that Benedetta was a deceiver? Two years had elapsed since she realized that Benedetta's death had been simulated, and even longer since she had discovered the true nature of her miraculous ring. Perhaps she was afraid of Benedetta, the abbess, rather than Splenditello. As abbess, Benedetta was a powerful figure, who could grant favors and punish almost at will, especially in this situation, in which the convent's confessor lacked a strong, independent character. Bartolomea's insistence that she was an unwilling participant, repeatedly forced to submit, may contain more than a grain of truth. She could well have been the helpless victim of sexual coercion.

Bartolomea, however, had strong reasons to represent her relationship in this light. Her statements were made to a tribunal that would certainly view the acts she described as very serious offenses—offenses that both lay and ecclesiastical courts sometimes punished by death. Her testimony was undoubtedly conditioned by what she believed would be least damaging to her own cause. Bartolomea may have been young and impressionable, but she also possessed "a sharp intelligence and wit," according to one of the nuns who knew her.[20] When we compare what she said in 1623 with the statements she made four years earlier to the provost, the differences are striking. The language of violence and fear, so prevalent in the latter account, is totally absent from the earlier one. At that time, when she was asked whether she was afraid during her nightly vigils with Benedetta, she had answered "When I was there [by her bed], I was not afraid, but felt happiness."[21] Her statements to the provost in

1619 also made it amply clear that she often approached Benedetta's bed voluntarily and that on her own initiative, to help her steady herself in her battles with the devil, she sometimes put her hand on her breast or embraced her.

Bartolomea was implicated in the relationship more deeply than she cared to admit. The ambivalence of her statements most likely reflects the inner turmoil of her own feelings as much as her desire to protect herself from the ecclesiastical authorities. Her relationship may have elicited fear and shame but also feelings of deep attraction—attraction first to a supernatural being who promised unimaginably wonderful favors, whether demonic or divine; and attraction later to an older woman whose power, education, and personal magnetism held forth the possibility of a richer and more rewarding emotional life. For the physical intimacy and sexual pleasure of the relationship could not be separated from all its other elements. To be loved, to be wanted, to be caressed and kissed, whether by angel or human, this surely bound Bartolomea to Benedetta by a deeply felt need for warmth and companionship.

Did Benedetta share such longings with her young lover? The ecclesiastical record suggests that she did. As Splenditello, Benedetta claimed to be "melting for love" of Bartolomea. She "promised to be her beloved" and repeatedly entreated her companion to pledge eternal love in return. She did not just offer love, she wanted to be loved herself. And what she sought in the relationship was more than sexual gratification. She wanted love in every sense, so that her words of love are as revealing of her desires as was her sexual passion. Deprived at a tender age of the love and protection of her parents, and especially of her father, to whom she had been deeply attached, forbidden by the rules of cloistered life to forge other ties of family or special friendship, Benedetta searched for affection elsewhere and found it in the arms of Bartolomea.

Yet unlike her companion, Benedetta refused to discuss her feelings about her relationship with the authorities, even if only to conceal them, as Bartolomea had tried to do. Throughout her interrogation, Benedetta was steadfast in her refusal to admit that she had engaged in sexual acts with Bartolomea. Her deeds and her words, and what can be surmised about the motives behind them, all come from Bartolomea's account. Had Benedetta remembered the relationship, her recollection would have been tantamount to an admission that she had participated in forbidden acts as herself rather than as an angel. This she couldn't do for her own self-protection. So long as Splenditello existed, either as a divine or a fallen angel, he, and not Benedetta, was responsible for the immodest deeds of which she was accused.

Splenditello turned out to be a useful character in more ways than one. First he deceived Bartolomea, now he might protect Benedetta from punishment. But does his usefulness mean that Benedetta intentionally refused to recall what happened? Was it that she wouldn't or that she couldn't remember? Did her refusal to acknowledge her sexual relationship grow out of a cynical desire to manipulate other people, or was it self-delusion? Perhaps Benedetta was just a good actress, taking her cue from the plays performed in Tuscan convents where nuns who dressed and talked like men played male parts.[22] So good was her performance that over a period of several years she managed to convince an entire convent, and many outsiders as well, that a beautiful male angel sometimes inhabited her body. But it is also possible that her purpose was to convince herself as well as others that she was Splenditello. The sheer effort of sustaining her performance intermittently over many years and the success with which she transformed her voice and her facial expression into that of the male angel point to the possibility that she was part of the intended audience. Benedetta may have been both deceiver and deceived in her self-created drama.[23]

What she concealed in her personification of male angel was not just her breach of the nun's vow of chastity, but her transgression of society's gender and sexual roles. Like the ecclesiastical authorities who heard the case, Benedetta lacked a cultural and intellectual framework to incorporate her behavior into her view of reality. Her preference for a sexual relationship with another woman, despite the fact that she could easily have secured male partners, as did other Pesciatine nuns, is not indicative of a clearly articulated choice. The only sexual relations she seemed to recognize were those between men and women. Her male identity consequently allowed her to have sexual and emotional relations that she could not conceive between women. But Benedetta was not an ordinary woman, she was a nun, and Splenditello could not be an ordinary male. He had to be an angel in order to be compatible with the sexual prohibitions imposed by the monastic vow. In this double role of male and of angel, Benedetta absolved herself from sin and accepted her society's sexual definitions of gender. Splenditello thus was essential to her sense of self because he allowed her to fashion an identity that at the same time assimilated and circumvented the values of patriarchal society. Through Splenditello, Benedetta could maneuver for a larger personal world within the limitations set by the social order.

Benedetta's difficulties in accepting her relationship with another woman were shared by the authorities in a different way. As if unable to comprehend fully what they had heard, rather than close the report with their account of her sexual offenses with Bartolomea, they added a kind of postscript about Benedetta's heterosexual misdeeds. As a final, and possibly more believable, seal on her sexual misbehavior, they wrote, "Let us add that which almost all the nuns affirm, that while . . . Sister Benedetta was abbess, she was at the grate a whole year, talking and laughing the whole day with a priest who is a distant relative, which caused great scandal and wonder among the laity and the nuns. . . . and to see and hear him better, she used a piece of iron to make four large holes in the grate, all right near each other." Benedetta and the priest did not try very hard to conceal their relationship. Witnesses testified that they were seen holding and kissing each other's hands "at all hours of the day and night." Their usual meeting places were either the little grated window through which the nuns received communion or the door of the convent. Occasionally, Benedetta was seen doing the same thing with another priest.

The authorities, of course, could not make a great deal of these meetings. Compared to the scandalous behavior between nuns and priests at some of the other convents in town, a few stolen kisses were not very serious. But these charges were important in that they helped to build the case for Benedetta's lack of virtue. Because church officials could not believe that a woman's sexual preferences might be directed solely at another woman, the relations between Benedetta and the priests made the other sexual charges more credible.

On this note, the report concluded. Having written it in the clearest and strongest way they knew, the clerical investigators returned to Florence and submitted it to the nuncio. How to handle the case from there on in would be up to him, and they hoped they would be left out of it.

If this was their fondest wish, alas, it did not come to pass. The wheels of the ecclesiastical bureaucracy ground on slowly. The nuncio had to be absolutely certain of all aspects of the case before he felt confident about making the right decision. As far as we know, he had no complaints with the report he received, but, to be doubly sure, he asked for one quick and final observation. The clerics returned to Pescia, and on November 5, 1623, submitted what they confidently called their "Last Report."

Their first finding was that since the time they had last seen Benedetta, all traces of the stigmata and the ring had disappeared. Moreover, when she was asked about "her angels, visions, apparitions, revelations, and ecstasies," Benedetta answered that she no longer saw any of them. Second, she apparently now agreed that she had been deceived by the devil. As a result, the investigators concluded that "all the things that were done in her or by her, not only those which are deemed sinful, but also the other deeds which were held to be supernatural and miraculous were done without her consent or her will, since they were done while she was out of her senses by the work of the devil."

Finally, Benedetta now lived the life of an obedient nun under the care of a new abbess. The investigators heard that she spent her time in works of humility, that she led a quiet life, attending divine services, and that she set a good example for all the other nuns.

This remarkable transformation seems to have occurred just in the nick of time. Benedetta may have realized that her days as a visionary were numbered. She had lost her hold on the nuns of her convent and she had no influential supporters left. Her only hope was to change her behavior, to follow the path of a good nun rather than that of a saint. She would have to blend into the anonymity of the convent and its routines, hence her turn toward works of humility and the quiet fulfillment of monastic duties.

The first step toward a new kind of life was to disavow her previous claims to being a recipient of divine favors. The essence of her predicament was how to do that without conceding to charges of deception. The solution was inherent in the structure of interpretations offered in her

own testimony and in the opinions of the nuncio's emissaries. From the very first report they wrote, they had
advanced the possibility that Benedetta may have been
the victim of the devil. Her reported ability to speak during her visions in a variety of languages and dialects that
were generally unknown to her, her flair for reading people's minds, her incapacitating illnesses, and her hereditary links to the devil, all pointed in the direction of
demonic obsession rather than simple fraud. She herself
had never fully rejected that possibility in her dealings
with any of the ecclesiastical authorities. Her only claim
had been that despite her doubts about the origins of her
visions and the supernatural signs on her body, she had
an overpowering belief that they came from God. Now
this belief disintegrated in the face of official opposition
and was replaced by Benedetta's acceptance of the demonic provenance of her mystical experiences. As a consequence, she could redouble her efforts to repress her
visions and eventually succeeded.[24]

This shift required a less drastic restructuring of self-
perception and social identity than any other alternative.
Because she was deceived by the devil, she could not be
fully accountable for her actions. Demonic possession and
obsession, unlike witchcraft, were considered involun-
tary. Benedetta had not made a conscious pact with the
devil, but was one of his victims. Confronted by such a
powerful and clever adversary, even the most reluctant
person might be seduced by his promises and false miracles. Consequently, she could accept that the supernatural events that took place and the sinful acts in which
she participated were the work of the devil because "they
were done," as the authorities stated, "without her consent and will."

Yet, even in the early seventeenth century, when the
presence and resourcefulness of the devil appeared to
contemporaries to have grown to ever greater propor-

tions, there were limits to his power. One of these limits was the individual's free will, whose existence the Catholic Church had just recently reaffirmed at the Council of Trent.[25] In addition, although traces of the devil were seen with increasing frequency in all the calamities that befell mankind, theologians did not see him as an omnipotent creature, else he would be the equal of God. The devil could only operate through God's permission, either to punish sinners or to test the strength of their will. A virtuous person might have stronger defenses against the devil's wiles than a person who did not lead a very upright life. There was, thus, a considerable amount of ambiguity in the Church's position on possession or vexing by a devil. On the one hand, the person that was assailed by the devil was not fully responsible for the diabolical acts committed through him; on the other, he was not totally blameless.

While the ecclesiastical investigators who wrote the last report on Benedetta seemed disposed toward leniency and emphasized her lack of consent and will, the final judgment need not necessarily absolve her from guilt. It would be up to the nuncio to determine in which direction the sentence and punishment would go.

Epilogue

THE STORY OF BENEDETTA CARLINI is shrouded in mystery for the next forty years. No records exist of the nuncio's pronouncements, and it is only the chance survival of a fragment of one nun's diary that allows us to know the outcome. On August 7, 1661, that nun, whose name has not come down to us, wrote in her diary: "Benedetta Carlini died at age 71 of fever and colic pains after eighteen days of illness. She died in penitence, having spent thirty-five years in prison."[1]

What led to Benedetta's imprisonment within the convent is a matter for conjecture. The words in the diary suggest that Benedetta was not imprisoned until 1626, three years after the "last report" was written. This gap is probably not the result of a casual mistake made by a nun writing about events that took place long before. The writer was very precise about her dates and figures—she recorded Benedetta's date of death and her exact age, without rounding it off, as was the customary practice. She also noted the precise number of days of Benedetta's last illness and remarked that she was the fourteenth nun to have died in the convent. Given such a concern for figures, she was not likely to make a mistake about when Benedetta was imprisoned.

Why it took so long to do this, however, is another matter. Perhaps the bureaucracy was simply slow. Perhaps Benedetta could not remain an obedient nun for long and after the investigators left and time elapsed, Splenditello emerged once more, thereby pushing the authorities toward a decision they had not originally intended to make. Perhaps, however, Benedetta wished to lead the life of an ordinary nun but the public following she had previously gained would not allow a return to anonymity. The diarist who recorded Benedetta's death remarked that "she was always popular among the laity," so that it may be that as long as she remained an integral part of her monastic community she was seen by the authorities as a threat to the established order. Nothing short of imprisonment within the walls of the convent would alleviate the problem.

But if the reasons for the apparent delay are unknowable, there is no doubt that the authorities considered the case of Benedetta Carlini a matter of public concern. When the nuncio's emissaries completed their second lengthy report of their findings, the nuncio sent a copy to the young grand duke, Ferdinand II, and his mother, the grand duchess Christina.[2] In the seventeenth century, the political and the religious order were closely intertwined.

Because the official decision about Benedetta's imprisonment has not survived, it is impossible to say with certainty what aspects of the case were most important in determining the sentence. As harsh as it may seem, it could be argued that Benedetta got off lightly. If the authorities had concluded that her crime was sodomy, they could have recommended that both she and Bartolomea be burnt at the stake. During the previous century, several women had been executed for sodomitical offenses throughout Europe. The jurist Prospero Farinacci recalled that as a youth in Rome he had seen women burned at the Campo di Fiori for acts of heterosexual sodomy. The Spanish jurist Antonio Gomez wrote of two nuns who were burned in sixteenth-century Spain. France also was the site of a few executions for sodomy: one woman was burned alive in 1535 and another was hanged in 1580. Another woman lost her life in mid-sixteenth century Geneva for "a crime so horrible that it cannot be named."[3]

Yet, despite these executions, there were often discrepancies between the letter of the law and its implementation. In most of the cases that ended in a death sentence there were what the authorities perceived as aggravating circumstances. In some, as in the Spanish case and one of the French cases, the women had "by illicit devices, supplied the defects of [their] sex." The use of such "material instruments" was for many officials the worst possible sodomitical act. In other cases, one of the partners in the relationship had attempted to live and dress like a man. This was a more dangerous crime than ordinary sodomy, for transvestism struck at the very heart of European gender and power relations.[4] By dressing like men, such women were attempting to sever the bonds that held them to the female sphere of the social hierachy. And, more important, they were attempting to usurp the functions of men. The result was that such "males," and not their female partners, tended to incur the greater wrath of the authorities. Their executions were thus necessary to protect the existing forms of social organization.[5]

But ordinary lesbian sexuality did not usually result in such repressive measures. In Granada, for example, several women were flogged and sent to the galleys for crimes similar to those committed by Benedetta and Bartolomea. Elsewhere women might simply be banished. Compared to these cases, where the sexual offenses were similar, Benedetta's treatment by the authorities appears much more severe.

It is likely therefore that the stiff penalty Benedetta received was not linked primarily to her sexual transgressions but rather to her monastic status, her claims to
miraculous favors, and her notoriety. Other nuns of her
time, who had not engaged in sexual misconduct but
who had achieved great fame and influence because of
their mystical claims, received similar sentences after they
were exposed as frauds or as victims of demonic deceptions. Their very success prior to their downfall in a sense
dictated their punishment. Because they had been perceived as holy women, they had gained a popular following and in a few instances even influenced the decisions
of popes and kings.[6] The greater their ability to deceive,
the greater the danger to the political and social order.
Such women had to be isolated from the rest of society
so as not to infect others with their erroneous beliefs.
They also had to be treated severely as a warning to other
women who might try to gain power over others through
similar means.

That these considerations may have influenced the authorities in Benedetta's case gains credence from the rather
different manner in which they handled Bartolomea's sexual misconduct. Our knowledge on this point again comes
from the diary of the anonymous nun. On 18 September,
1660, she wrote: "Sister Bartolomea [blank] died [today?];
when Sister Benedetta Carlini was engaged in those deceits noted in this book on page [blank], she was her
companion and was always with her. And because of this
she experienced many difficulties. . . . In temporal affairs
she worked as hard as she could and in spiritual affairs
she was very devoted and totally given over to holy prayer."
There was no mention of imprisonment, and the description of Bartolomea's activities suggests that she engaged
in the usual routines of convent life. Bartolomea may have
been stigmatized for a time by the other nuns and may
have had to endure occasional reminders of her misdeeds,

but she appears to have spent her life as an ordinary nun. The authorities may have believed her version of what happened and may have treated her like a gullible victim of an elaborate deception. But even if they harbored suspicions about the willingness of her involvement, there was no danger either for the nuns or for the outside community in allowing her to continue living in their midst.

Benedetta, however, was a much greater threat. With her the ecclesiastical officials followed the dictates of St. Teresa, who, in mid-sixteenth century, had written: "It is the gravest of faults if any nun falls into the sin of sensuality and is convicted or seriously suspected of such a thing . . . Let such sisters be put in prison . . . a sister who commits sins of the flesh shall be imprisoned for life . . . [and] shall in no case, even though she repent and implore mercy and pardon, be received back into the community, save if some reasonable cause supervene and on the recommendation and advice of the visitor."[7] In Benedetta's case, apparently no such recommendation was made.

What prison life was like, we can well imagine from a variety of sources. "No sister in prison must be spoken to by any nun, save those who act as her wardens," St. Teresa commanded. "Nor must they send her anything under pain of suffering the same penalty."[8] A sister in prison should have her veil and scapular taken away. She should be let out only to hear mass and to follow the other nuns to where they disciplined themselves with their whips. On those days she might be allowed to eat on the floor of the refectory, near the door, so that the others might step over her as they left the room. Several times a week she should receive only bread and water for sustenance.[9]

For Benedetta death must have been a release from the torment of her life. But it also marked her re-entry into the community of the living. "Once dead," wrote the nun in her diary, "they brought her into the church as they do with the other nuns and dressed her with the black veil and habit worn by the others."

Word of her death spread quickly outside the convent walls, and the collective memory of a small town was stirred. Forty years after the events that had brought her notoriety, the power of her personality could still move those around her. "As she was always popular among the laity," wrote the nun in her diary, "when they heard of her death they created much agitation while the body was still unburied and it was necessary to bar the doors of the church to avoid any uproar and tumult until the burial."

What brought people to the gate of the convent thirty-five years after Benedetta was placed in solitary confinement? Perhaps the reason was that her prophetic warnings to those who refused to believe in her had finally come to pass and in 1631 the plague did indeed strike Pescia, leaving behind a shrunken population and empty houses where thriving families had once lived. Perhaps it was that the people had never really believed in the officials' efforts to discredit her miracles. Whatever the reason, ordinary people wanted to see and touch her body, or even to take some of it with them like the relics of a saint. In the end, Benedetta triumphed. She had left her mark on the world and neither imprisonment nor death could silence her.

APPENDIX

A Note About the Documents,
with Selected Translations

The reconstruction of Benedetta Carlini's story is based
in large measure on a file of documents entitled *Miscellanea
Medicea* 376, insert 28, found in the State Archive of Florence. The materials in this file consist primarily of abbre-
viated transcripts, letters, and summaries of documents
that are no longer extant. Some of the file's contents have
survived in more than one copy. Some are undated and
can only be placed in the proper temporal and institutional
framework from internal evidence. This is not unusual
for premodern sources but it does raise difficulties, some
of them insurmountable, in the use and interpretation of
the documents.

Even with the greatest care, it is not always possible to
determine the exact date of a particular document or for
whom it was written. It is also difficult to discern the
voices of the protagonists from transcripts that are not
verbatim, but are filtered through scribes' efforts to convey
the sense of a witness' statements. Sometimes it is obvious
that despite a third-person rendering, a witness' words
are captured verbatim or close to it. Sometimes in his
hurry, a scribe might lapse into the first person, giving a
closer sense of the sound of the original. This and the

fact that witnesses were asked to verify the accuracy of the written record can give us some confidence in getting nearer to what was actually said. Nonetheless, it is important to remember that in all instances the words recorded are at best conveyed secondhand.

Another difficulty is that it is not always possible to tell the difference between fact and fiction as conventionally defined. For example, some of the "facts" about Benedetta's life—her difficult birth, her special relationship to wondrous animals during her childhood—are based on the testimony of witnesses who heard her give an account of her own life while she was in a trance. Some of these events could be corrobrated by others who knew Benedetta at the time they were said to have taken place, although it is not clear from the records whether such verification was sought for all the events related. Other events, which were unwitnessed, were unverifiable. But whether dealing with events for which corroboration was found or not, their great similarity with episodes in folk tales and saints' lives suggests that Benedetta and those who recalled them were modeling them on certain narrative and literary genres. Fact blended into fiction, just as life imitated art. Yet for some, though not all, purposes these distinctions are not significant. Indeed, it could be argued that to impose twentieth-century notions of fiction on seventeenth-century notions of reality is in itself to create a historical fiction. Whether the events did or did not take place, the undeniable fact is that contemporaries thought they did.

Because of these and other complexities mentioned previously in the text, it is hoped that the annotated list of pertinent documents contained in *Misc. Med.* 376, ins. 28, and the translated selections that follow will help the reader see the process of recreation from document to historical narrative.

Annotated list of documents in Misc. Med. 376, ins. 28:

"Virtues of the True Religious"—undated spiritual guide for nuns.

Untitled document containing the results of fifteen ecclesiastical interrogations made between 27 May, 1619 and 26 July, 1620. A few selections are translated below.

"Brief discourse of the things that are said about the Mother, Sister Benedetta Carlini of Vellano of the Theatines of Pescia"—undated report critical of Benedetta. Probably written sometime between August 1622 and March 1623. The early date is suggested both by the fact that it refers to a previous trial (*processo*), and that in a later document in which the "Brief Discourse" is mentioned by title, it is said to have been compiled at the behest of Alfonso Giglioli, who became nuncio in August 1622. As for the late date, the report's mention of Father Ricordati in the present tense locates it prior to October 1623. Moreover, the lack of evidence about Benedetta's sexual relations and fraudulent stigmata as well as the tentative tone of the conclusions suggest it was written prior to reports that mention those aspects of the case. And since internal evidence in those documents date them to sometime after March 1623, it is likely that the "Brief discourse" was written before that.

"Abstract of the Trial of Benedetta"—undated report stamped with the nuncio's seal. Written after March 1623 because it records that two years before, on the day of the Annunciation, Benedetta encountered the soul of her dead father. Giuliano was still alive in November 1620. The end date is that of the "Final Report."

"Account of the visit made to the Theatine nuns, also

known as Holy Mary of Pescia"—undated account, probably written as a preliminary set of findings to be
incorporated into the "Abstract of the Trial of Benedetta." As can be seen from the following transla-
tion, the account emphasizes the evidence of fraud
and immoral conduct.

"Last Report"—dated 5 November, 1623.

Letter from the nuncio to two Capuccin Fathers, wishing them well on their assigned task. Dated 13 December, 1623.

Letter from the nuncio to the above regarding the difficulties of finding a confessor for the Theatines. Dated
17 December, 1623.

Report to "Your Serene Highnesses"—undated summary of the major findings of the "Abstract of the
trial of Benedetta." Presumably written some time
after that document.

Selections from the First Investigation

On the twenty-seventh day of May, 1619

On the first visit, the provost saw on the hands, feet, and
side of Benedetta signs of dry blood as large as a *crazia*
[a small Tuscan coin]; and when they were washed with
warm water, one could see a small cut from which blood
ran out; in several places on the head one could see many
signs of dry blood like the blood on the hands; and when
they were washed with warm water, one could see in the
places that had been washed, punctures from which blood
poured out and which remained on the cloth with which
she was dried.

Benedetta confesses that on the second Friday of Lent
of the year 1619, while in bed between two and three
hours of the night [7 to 8 P.M.] the thought came to her

to suffer all the things suffered by Jesus Christ; and there appeared in front of her a crucified man as large as a good sized man, and he was alive and asked her if she were willing to suffer for his love because he was Jesus Christ; and she protested that if this were an illusion of the Devil she did not want to consent and would tell her Spiritual Father [her confessor] and she made the sign of the cross. He assured her that he was God and that he wanted her to suffer for the duration of her life, that she should arrange herself in the form of a cross because he wanted to imprint his holy wounds in her body. When she did this, a flash burst forth from all of them, which she thought imprinted themselves on her hands. And on her head she saw many small rays that seemed to delineate her entire head and she felt great pains in it and in her hands. But afterwards a great contentment came into her heart. The large rays she saw were five, but those of the head were a great many more, but small ones; that she did not arrange her feet one on top of the other, but found them wounded and arranged without realizing it; and she felt pain there. On Sundays they seem to be numb; on Mondays and Tuesdays she feels little or no pain; on all other days great pain; on Fridays more than any other days and on that day there is more bleeding, except for this morning as you have seen.

On the fourteenth day of June, 1619

On the third visit one could see the dried blood on the left hand and foot. And when they were washed one could see the cut, from which oozed a bit of fresh blood, which when dried, flowed into the towel; and on her head the signs and holes that seemed healed eight days ago were full of small amounts of dry blood; and when her hair was cut with scissors, one could see many signs of fresh blood that went all the way around her head;

and since she was ordered to wash the blood from her head, she retired to a room to reclose her habit. Suddenly she turned around and going towards them with her hands to her head and her face down, she said, "Jesus, what is this?" And one could see from a puncture of the head the blood instantly spilling on her face and on to the ground; and she showed signs of pain and when the blood was dried with a towel, it stopped.

On the eighth day of July, 1619

On the sixth visit, on the right hand one could see blood in the cut ——— — feet without blood; on the head a little bit; the side was not seen, but she says that it is as before. She adds that one morning when she was praying she found herself in a beautiful and agreeable garden with many flowers and fruits; in which there was a fountain with beautifully scented water which gushed out of a gold spigot; there was an Angel dressed in a green garment full of small gold crosses. He had white and gilded wings and in his hand he held a sign whose large gold letters proclaimed: "Whosoever wants to take water from this fountain, let him purge his cup or not come nearer." And because she did not understand, the Angel on his own volition told her, "if you want to know God, lift all earthly desires from your heart." And without answering she felt in her heart a great desire to detach herself from the world; and she came to and did not see anything else. When she was abstracted from her senses, she felt violently drawn. No one led her to the garden, but she suddenly found herself there. And it was four or five years ago, since the building of the convent had not yet started. And it seems that this vision took place place before the vision of the fiery rays. She does not remember what she was doing when she had this vision. Before she had not had any thought of such a garden nor read about it in a book.

She did not gather flowers or fruits in the garden nor did she drink water. When she first saw herself alone she felt fear, then contentment. She is amazed to remember it since she had not thought of it until now; and she feels as if she is present there. She does not remember how long the vision lasted. When she came to, she seemed to feel totally happy, with a desire to be better than before.

On the seventh of the present month of July 1619, I got down on my knees to pray that I not be deceived by the Devil but rather that I die first. And suddenly, before she became aware of it, the Angel who used to appear in front of her took her to a church where she thought she heard Mass and the priest who was at the altar turned to her and reassured her, telling her on behalf of Jesus Christ that she was not deceived by the Devil and he invited her to receive the Holy Sacrament, which he wanted to administer to her with his own hands. She forced herself not to go to him, but the Angel took her by the hand and brought her there; and she got on her knees and he gave her communion; and afterwards the Angel took her back to her own place. There he made her sit down and the priest said to her that she should be strong in all adversity and temptation, that in the end, thanks to God, she would have visions; and that she should wait only for help from Jesus Christ, telling her that he was St. Peter, who had done all this at the command of Jesus. This gave her great contentment and interior peace, that never in her life had she felt this . . .

. . . To obey her Spiritual Father, she prayed to God that He send her travails instead of ecstasies and revelations, since it seemed to her that this would be safer against the deceits of the devil. And her prayer was heard, her bodily pains having started four years ago. But for almost the last two years they have been greater than in the first two since they come over her entire body, starting in the evening, and they last about six to eight hours in

which there often appear young men armed with rough
swords in hand to kill her. Other times they beat her
giving her great pain over her entire body. Another time
there came one young man with a ring to tell her that he
wanted her to be his bride and she answered him that
she wanted to be the bride of Jesus. He wanted to put
the ring on her finger by force, telling her companion to
hold her hand. Other times they told her not to stay in
this place, that she would become ill and that in the end
she would not be certain of her salvation. And they said
other things which she cannot remember. And this struggle, involving many temptations with these young men,
lasted many times. [They told her] that she shouldn't
persevere here but that she should leave, that this would
be better for me. It seemed to her that she saw them
infallibly, as she sees your Reverence. She seemed to
recognized some, but she did not look at them except
when she couldn't help it. And that they were from Pescia
and she knew one from when he was small. She knew
the one that wanted to marry her. They seemed handsome
to her, but she didn't want to look at them. She hid from
them and felt the pain of the beatings she received. It
seemed to her that they pursued her with iron chains,
sticks, and other objects, and swords in hand. She felt all
bruised, but she did not see if she had bruises on her
body. She never wanted that young man to touch her
hand to put the ring on it. She was in bed when she saw
them; and the pains that came from them were the worst
she had, having them usually in the evening; and at first
she didn't have them, but later they became worse. For
two continuous winter nights they beat her, and they
continued at other times, often in the summer. . . . She
does not recall that they said anything to her, except for
the one with the ring, but they spoke among themselves.
Before the incident with the ring they beat her, and the
one with the ring is always the first to beat her and is

more presumptuous than the others and stronger at beating her. On the evening that he came to put the ring on her, he did not beat her at first, but came with much pretence and he spoke with the others; and it seemed that he wanted to do as she wished, that he would not alter her will; and because she did not want to consent, he turned to her enraged in order to beat her with all the others, he being the first. She does not recall that they said anything the first time she saw them, but it seemed to her they came with deceit and wanted to approach her with a certain deceitful look. And since she recognized that this is a trick of the Devil's, she turned the other way so as not to see them, and when they approached her, they came to her side even more enraged. She realized that they came to her side with a pleasing face and she turned so as not to see them, and she seemed to hear a voice that said she should not pay attention to them but should drive them away from her. And she saw them as a real presence not in her imagination. It seemed to her that they remained with her too long. The pains ceased gradually when they left. When she saw them appear, she would make the sign of the cross on her heart and it seemed to her that after doing this, they came nearer. . . . They seemed to be dressed in yellow-red gowns, and the one with the ring was dressed more neatly and handsomely than the others. And it seemed that he incited the others to beat her; without him it seemed they did nothing. It seemed to her that there were four or five who beat her but all had companions; the former being the main ones but all beat her. And one time more of them came than ever, and she made the sign of the cross many times, and they could not come nearer, and they became more enraged and beat her harder than ever. Since they were two or three yards away, she did not know what they had in their hands, but although they started out handsome they turned ugly. And they beat her until the dawn bell, close to three or four hours of the night. She remained still and she seldom sent for another sister in order not to disturb anyone. At other times, the young men left enraged, but not as ugly as these last; this was in the winter. It seemed that they ceased to come before last Lent but she does not remember well. It seems that the last time they beat her and did not say anything. When they stopped coming, she felt little pain, and they stopped at Lent. She does not remember the day. And the pains stopped when the signs appeared, having at that time had few. And the worst pain was felt the evening that she received those signs, when she seemed to be beside herself (*altratta*). She does not remember having had either ecstasies or revelations during the pains.

On the 23rd day of July, 1619

On the tenth visit, one could see blood coming out of the top side of both hands, and when they were dried one could see the blood stains imprinted on the kerchief that was used for that purpose. The blood was not visible on the feet because she said that she dried it in the morning. Fresh blood could be seen on her side, and when it was dried with a cloth, there remained a good quantity imprinted on it. The head could be seen with a bit of dried blood. And when she was made to take off her coif, one could see only one bleeding puncture, and when Your Holiness touched it with a cloth, a bit of blood impressed itself on it. Other punctures could not be seen because they were covered by hair and it did not seem right for the moment to have the hair removed. . . .

After lengthy testimony from Benedetta Carlini and the Abbess Felice di Giovanni Guerrini, there follows the testimony of Mea [Bartolomea] di Domenico Crivelli:

Mea di Domenico Crivelli, under oath—The day of the
Holy Trinity I found myself in the choir along with the
others who were present at the wedding. I had not been
present to hear Benedetta when she was in ecstasy and
said that she would be married on that day because I was
in bed sick; and I got up, having been told about this
marriage by the other girls. On that day I heard and saw
the following: we went to the choir all in order and she
picked up a basket of flowers and scattered them all over
the choir;   and after that she lit all the candles and
gave one to each of us. She took the crucifix and began
to intone *Gesu corona virginum*. We went on procession
and when we returned to the choir she began the litanies
of the Madonna, and when they were finished Benedetta
rose, scattering incense mostly over the small altar, then
on the other parts of the room. Afterwards she got down
on her knees and bowed three times, first to the altar,
then to the south side of the choir, then to the north side.
Then, in a low voice, she intoned to herself the *Veni creator
Spiritus*, although it was heard by all as music, so soft
was her voice; and two other hymns after these, but it
was not possible to hear what hymns they were because
they were softer than the previous ones. But those who
know how to read, are under the impression that they
were things in Latin, then she placed herself at the side
of the crucifix mentioned below. There she remained for
some time, and lifting her head she remained rather still.
Then she said certain words that I don't remember well:
"Jesus, I am not worthy." And I saw that she lifted her
arm and her right hand and the fourth finger, and shortly
afterwards I saw that she kissed that finger and I heard
that she thanked God with many words for the benefit
done to her. Then I heard her say: "I want to have her
sit on that middle chair and to explain her whole life."
And she quickly rose and she sat on that middle chair.
And she said that the lights she had lit symbolized the

33 years that Our Lord lived in this world, and the three
largest ones were the three years closest to his death; the
thickest candle, which was golden and had two knots,
signified his great charity for the health of mankind; the
other large one, the great charity of the Madonna; thus
he said that while she lived, he wanted her to pray for
all. Those lights she gave us symbolized the virtues that
we should derive from her, that it should be like a spur
to divine service. The twelve gloves signified the twelve
Apostles; the color green, the great hope that she always
placed in me; red the love that she always wants to have
for me; blue the exertion of always having the mind on
the things of heaven; the earthen floor, that just as we
should be dead to the things of this world, so I wanted
the floor covered so that the earth not be seen; the red
silk flowers, the saintly virtues that we should derive from
her. She does not remember anything else about the wedding arrangements. In talking about her life she talked
about the time when her heart was removed, when he
gave her the signs on the hands, feet, side, and head;
that he wanted that she be a true portrait of him. Neither
did he want her to hide them but that they be known.
And that she would not be believed the first or the second
or the third time. And I will allow this for her merit, and
I want her to prepare herself because I want to avail myself
of her in all that pleases me. She spoke further about the
comet that we saw this year over the monastery but I
can't remember the details; and that he wanted our monastery to be like the sea, which retains the bodies of the
dead only for three days and he wanted to send temptations to those among us who did not want to travel the
road to perfection, so that they would become desperate
and leave by themselves. . . . And that there would be
some that would not believe her and for that he wanted
to punish them and he wanted her to warn those in the
convent that spoke among themselves on account of van-

ity, and when he spoke of vanities, she would raise her voice turning towards the windows that faced outside of the monastery. She said so many things that I get confused and I don't know what to say. She does not recall that Benedetta said anything when she raised her hand; and when she kissed her finger she didn't say anything. When she said these things, she was not herself because that voice did not sound like hers. She had her eyes open, but lowered. She never got up from that chair while she spoke. Then after she finished she raised herself up and got on her knees and remained there for perhaps a half hour; then she got up. We put out all the lights. She was in the choir, back to herself and still. We left the choir and she was totally happy. That day the wife of the previous Vicar was there; she was outside the choir; and when Benedetta went there she said some words to her. Benedetta spoke for about three hours and when she finished the 23rd hour had sounded. She never said anything about this wedding.

On the first day of August, 1619

This visit begins with the testimony of the Abbess Felice and Sister Angelina and is followed by the testimony of Mea Crivelli, excerpted below:

The above-mentioned Mea, under oath—She sleeps next to the superior, Felice; and last year next to Benedetta; and I began to sleep next to Felice when we came here last November, if I'm not mistaken. When we came up here I put myself near the large window and Benedetta was here below near the door, but because she was in pain at night, I went to stay down there with her so that I could get up and help her. And often I did not go to sleep at night until the eighth or ninth hour [1 or 2 A.M.] so that I could help her because she had those pains. She had those pains in her heart and often throughout her entire body, but the former were the strongest. And I know it because she had me put my hand on her heart because she seemed to feel less pain that way. And while I had my hand there it felt as if a dagger were hitting it, so strong was it. And with my hand in place she seemed to flail around less but when I didn't have my hand there, she would not stay in bed because of the great pains she experienced. And I would work so hard that I would sweat. The pains lasted two years, and during a period of four months they were continuous. And it seemed to her that they went away in November. And they would start at 24 hours and last until 9 or 10 hours [2 or 3 A.M.]. But during the day she did not have them. She did not know what caused them. When she had them she moaned softly and kept her mouth closed so as not to bother the others. Since Ember days of Spring she no longer has the pains. Sometimes she would call me twice a night because she was still mindful of the dead abbess. She would tell her, "hold me, help me," and as soon as I heard her I would put my hand on her heart and would quiet her. And she would tell me this because she could not hold still on account of her great pains. She never told me what caused them, but when I would say that Jesus wanted to test her, she would confirm it. And when she had these pains one could smell an awful sulphurous stink coming out of her mouth. At night I never saw anyone appear in front of her. But I heard her talk; I heard her say that she did not want to leave this place but that she would rather be ill for love of Jesus and she answered the same thing many times. And she wanted to persevere in this monastery. And when she touched her heart she never heard her say anything else, except when Jesus took out her heart. I went to her and I put my hand on the side of her heart. I seemed to feel a hole. Benedetta's heart was removed and I thought to myself that it was Jesus that did it. The night of the second day of Easter, her heart was removed after the same hour as her signs had appeared. Because I found myself present and heard her, she began to speak and said that she saw Jesus approaching, "but I don't know if it is the devil's work, pray to God for me." (Benedetta confessed this but these words were left.) "If it is the devil's work, I will make the sign of the cross on my heart and he will disappear." Shortly thereafter, she began to laugh and became all happy. And I heard her saying, "What would you do my Jesus! You came to take my heart but I don't want to do it without permission from my Spiritual Father." And then I heard her say, "You will see that he will have no objections. Do it." And I saw that she laid down on her back and said, "where will you take my heart from?" And I heard her say, "from the side." And I saw that she suffered a great deal of pain and I heard her say, "Oh my Jesus, show it to me. That is it. No wonder I felt such pain." And I heard her say, "I would like it as a sign of your love and in conformity with your will, but how can I live without a heart now that you have left me without one? How will I be able to love you?" And I saw all these things because I was there by the bed, secretly. But she didn't see me because when I realized that she was returning to her senses, I retreated behind the curtain so she wouldn't see me. I realized that she was not herself because she seemed like one who dreams and this was very obvious. And she would have sent me away and she wouldn't have spoken in this manner. And I touched her near the heart and one could feel an empty space and she remained there apparently out of her senses. She did not say anything because I pretended to cover her and to arrange her sheets. I made the sign of the cross, and I always did it although I had no fear. I did not say anything about this because I didn't see it, but knew that for God it is not impossible to live without a heart. She was without it for three days. I was present when he put it back in and I think it was the second hour of the night, when she had gone to bed. And I went to see if she needed anything and she said I should go to bed, that she had no needs. I didn't want to leave and indeed I couldn't leave, feeling as if I were being held. I would have wanted to obey, but feeling that I couldn't leave, I pulled the curtain of her bed and placed myself behind it. And shortly thereafter I heard her begin to say, "Oh what lovely company; oh, how they come in order;" and that they should make themselves comfortable around the bed. I saw her with her eyes lowered as if fearing to look at them, and I heard her say, "Beautiful young woman, tell me please what is your name?" And she asked this twice. And the woman replied, "Catherine." Then she asked what so many people had come to do: "Don't you want to tell me? I want to know so that I can prepare myself." And she said, "Oh my bridegroom did you come to give me back my heart?" And she remained thus, a bit quiet. Then gaily she opened her arms as when people want to embrace each other, saying, "My Jesus, don't show it to me because I will lose my sight." And she turned her head in the other direction, saying that it was so beautiful that she couldn't watch it. And she asked him what those rays meant. "It is the capacity of your love. And that circle of gold is the conformity of your will. And it is just as I wanted it." And I heard her say: "Put it back in the same place that you took it from, but I don't want to disrobe here in the presence of so many people." And she retreated and she let go the cloths, uncovering her side, and I saw that the sign on her side was larger and redder than at other times. And I saw that she was very happy. And when He put it [the heart] inside her I began to see that the flesh rose up and she moved slowly, slowly with those rays in front; and all the ribs, which I could see, were lifted up. And when it arrived at the place where

the heart belongs, it stopped. And she slowly turned with
her forehead bent down and the heart reentered its place.
But it was so large that one could see it would never fit
and it raised her flesh. Then she covered herself up again,
but before she did that I touched it and it felt so large
and so hot that my hand could not stand it. And I heard
that she began to thank God with many words that I can't
remember, but among them I remember the following:
"Oh my Jesus what greater gift could you give me than
to have given me your own heart." And [she said] many
other things, thanking those saints, but I began to realize
that she wanted to return to herself again and I put myself
behind the curtain so that she wouldn't see me; and when
she returned to her senses she saw me and said: "There
you are; I didn't think that you would be here." And she
was completely happy. I asked her if she needed anything
and then I went to sleep. When I was there I did not have
any fear but rather contentment. Neither did I fear when
she was assailed and had those pains as when once I
found her saying, "Hold me because he wants to put the
ring on me, but I don't want to do it no matter what."
And so I went to hold her and I took her hand and she
thrashed around and it looked as if she would maim her
hands if I didn't hold her. And I heard her say, "I want
to be the bride of Christ not yours." I never saw anyone,
not even the person who gave her back the heart. I did
not see her heart either when it was taken from her or
when it was put back. I was present when she received
those signs because always at Lent around the second
hour, when she went to bed it seemed to me that she
fainted, but she stayed like this a while and then returned.
And I heard her begin to speak and she said, "O Lord I
would like to suffer to the point of death so that you may
grant me your grace, because on my own account I can
do nothing." And she said many other words that I can't
remember: "But my Jesus, you want to give me these

signs, but I don't want to do this without permission from my Spiritual Father." And I saw that she arranged herself in the form of the cross and became as red as a glowing ember and she said, "My Lord, there are others who are better than I; I don't deserve this since I am a sinner." And I could see that she suffered such pain in her hands, feet, and side, and remaining like this for a little while, she asked that I lift her by the arms because she couldn't do it by herself. And I lifted her and saw that she had some red marks like small rosettes on the hands, feet, and side. And she had a deep red band around her head, but it was bloodless. And then I left, but in any case I was there and pretended not to pay attention to her. I saw no one going to her side in the evenings. The evening before was the last time that she had pains and she said that they were the worst that she ever had. And on the same night that she received the signs, I had to help her because she felt as if she had a spear on her side that pierced her through and through. And this lasted a quarter of an hour, and afterwards she told me to leave her so that I would be in less discomfort. The signs came about a quarter of an hour later, and she was charged not to say anything to anyone about what she had seen or heard.

Benedetta in response [to questions] says, Jesus appeared before me with a drawn sword, and I never told anyone, but I can't remember the day exactly, but it seems to me that it was the month of June last, when I was in morning prayer. And it seemed to me that I saw Jesus in majesty, but angered, and he said to me that he was not finding anyone in this town, which was in such need, that would ask him for mercy. And I said to him that if he did not find anyone, I would be the one and if there were a need for it, I would stay in Purgatory until the day of judgment, on condition that I had been good. And I thought he said that I should hold him dear. And be-

cause of this I wanted to placate his ire. And while he
said this I realized what it was he wanted to say about a
punishment. And I thought he said a punishment of plague
if he were not placated with prayer. And he wanted that
there be processions with his image in front. And thus I
thought he said to me that I should always pray for him,
that there was a need for it. I arranged the procession
with permission from the Father Confessor. When I first
saw him I was fearful, then suddenly that passed. I was
certain that it was Jesus, seeing him in majesty. He had
a sword in hand and it seemed to me that it was bloody.
It appeared that he was accompanied by I don't know
how many angels, but I don't remember it very well. I
tried inwardly not to believe that it was for punishment,
but I couldn't help believing it. I felt a growing desire in
me to pray nonetheless, but as to the rest, [illegible]. It
seems that he showed great contentment when I began
to pray to him for the people of this town, and [he sug-
gested] that I continue. I was not then in my senses because I couldn't see the others at prayer. At first I didn't
think of anything other than the customary meditation on
when Jesus was tied to the column. I remember that one
morning when I was at prayer by myself in front of the
Madonna because I rose later than the others, I saw on
looking up that she had fallen on the small altar. And
she had her face outside the altar and I began to scream.
I called the Mother Superior and she ran over and set her
straight. At first, as near I can remember, I didn't look at
her, and a moment later I saw her fallen over. In the
evening the reading had been about when the Madonna
was in the temple and learned the virtues. And because
there was no one here at home who could teach me how
to read, and I had a great desire to learn, I prayed to the
Madonna that she should teach me. When I left home to
come to Pescia, my mother told me "leave me, who am
your mother; I want you to pick the mother of God for

your mother, because I have heard that those girls have a Madonna. In all your needs I want you to turn to her as you would to me." And when I arrived at the house, I told that Madonna that I wanted her for a mother and this I did and [she told me?] many other things that I should do but which I didn't. And the usual signs were examined and the ring in the same manner as above.

Account of the visit made to the Theatine Nuns,
also known as Holy Mary of Pescia

Sister Benedetta Carlini said in one of her ecstasies that when Jesus took her heart, she raised her sleeve up to mid-arm, and when he put the heart back he put it through her side and made it go through between the skin and the flesh on her chest until it arrived at its place, and it bulged out of her chest like a bread roll as it went along. This is stated by two nuns, one of whom says she was present and saw the heart when it was back in place up to one inch deep and saw that bread-like bulge on her chest. And both confirm that when he came to return the heart, he said that she should uncover herself and because she answered that she was ashamed to, he added where I am there is no shame. This she said in ecstasy.

One of her angels said in one of her ecstasies that since God eternal had elected her for his bride, when she was about to come up here [to the new monastery], he commanded all the angels of the Pesciatines to scatter flowers on the streets that she would pass and that they should welcome her, and that in ecstasy she saw not only the flowers scattered on the streets, but also all the angels bowing to her. Two nuns confirm what she said in ecstasy but they confess that they did not see flowers on any of the streets.

She said in ecstasy that God granted her the power to understand immediately what people were about to say as soon as they even uttered the first word. He also granted her the power to see into people's hearts. This was stated by only one nun.

While in ecstasy she revealed that the souls of some individuals had gone to paradise and she named some. Two [nuns] say this. And the first nun adds that one of these souls had received the right to be with her [Benedetta] always, and speaking through Benedetta it lamented not having known or seen Benedetta when it was alive.

She further revealed while in ecstasy that some souls had gone to purgatory and she specified the amount of time they had spent there before going to paradise. One nun said this.

She also said in ecstasy that she had received God's grace to help the souls that were near death and that she had taken many out of purgatory. And one morning, also in ecstasy, she showed how she took many from there, motioning with her hands as if she were taking them and telling the angels that they should carry them to paradise. She affirmed that she had received this privilege from God because of her new heart and added that she gave her blessing to those souls who had not finished their penance, and they felt great contentment and comfort from this because on her hands she had the wounds of Jesus Christ.

On the morning of St. John the Baptist, while in ecstasy, she assigned an angel to each of the nuns, in addition to their guardian angels, telling them the names and the order to which the angels belonged, all of which are written on a piece of paper. And this is affirmed by all the nuns. Both she and her companion have three angels each, as they themselves confess.

Benedetta's angels sermonized for two Lents on the gospel of the Mass of the day while the other nuns disciplined themselves. They exhorted the nuns to virtue and above all to obedience, poverty, and chastity. All say this, and they confirm that her angels call each other *Signore* and they are recognizable by the different dialects in which they speak—one in her maternal tongue, one in Florentine dialect and one in the dialect of Lucca.

She has been seen by two nuns renewing her wounds at various times with a large needle, as they themselves confess. And three other nuns state they have observed that her wounds sometimes seem very small and almost dry and later, after she has locked herself in her study for a while, they are fresh, as if they had been made recently.

Two nuns state that when she has her hair washed no puncture marks are left, and that her head remains clean. One of these nuns always does the washing and affirms that she has seen her locked in her study in front of a mirror, taking blood from her wound with a large needle and putting it on her head. And two nuns say they've observed that there were no visible puncture marks on her head and no broken skin, except at the start.

Three nuns report that she not only walks, but runs through the house, as if there were nothing wrong with her feet. One of these nuns once saw her jump down from a small table and heard her say, "Whoever saw me jump would say that there's nothing wrong with my feet." Another nun, whose turn it was to wash the wounds on her feet, never saw them or found any blood there.

Many times three nuns have noticed that the two fingers contiguous to the ring finger had the same color as the ring where the fingers touched. Many times the ring was faded in color so that it was almost invisible and after she locked herself in her study for a while, the color was bright. And one of these nuns, suspecting that she was making the ring with saffron, looked around and finally found in her desk, a small brass box containing some diluted saffron. Another nun observed that those small stones that are on the ring in the form of a cross are sometimes broken and sometimes whole so that she is suspicious, as was the other nun.

Almost all the nuns say they have twice seen gold on the wounds on her hands, and particularly on the morning of the resurrection, but two say that before [these events] she had locked herself in her study for a while. One of these nuns added that while the others were preparing themselves in the choir, Benedetta took some time to come down and always kept her hands under her gown and did not take them out until after receiving the sacraments. That gold was tinsel. Another nun saw in her study thin golden sheets that were left over from when some things were gilded in the choir.

Five nuns say they saw another ring, a yellow one with a red stone, on the index finger of her right hand. But one nun says that even the ring was red, and three others say that they saw another ring that was all yellow and without a stone on her middle finger. And two of these suspected that she herself made the ring with saffron and the stone with blood from her wound . . .

Almost all the nuns say that for a whole year while she was abbess, she spent the days at the grate talking and laughing with a priest, which caused great scandal and wonder among the laity and the nuns. And for this purpose she often left Vesper services. One nun adds that during the course of the winter, she saw her at the small communion window with that priest until three at night at least twice or three times a week and they held and kissed each other's hands. And she did the same thing many times at the door of the convent, while she stood straight and he was on his knees. Another nun confirms having seen them at the small window three or four times. And she was seen by a nun many times with another priest at the same window. Once, when this nun was left there by force while Benedetta went to run an errand, this priest asked her to put out her hand and when she refused, he started to put his inside but she closed the window on him just in time. Another nun states that on another occasion, the first priest went up on the altar and through the open grate that serves to see the holy sacrament when it is raised, spied into the choir to see who was there. This nun closed the grate on his face . . .

For two continuous years, two or three times a week, in the evening, after disrobing and going to bed waiting for her companion, who serves her, to disrobe also, she would force her into the bed and kissing her as if she were a man she would stir on top of her so much that both of them corrupted themselves because she held her by force sometimes for one, sometimes for two, sometimes for three hours. And [she did these things] during the most solemn hours, especially in the morning, at dawn. Pretending that she had some need, she would call her, and taking her by force she sinned with her as was said above. Benedetta, in order to have greater pleasure, put her face between the other's breasts and kissed them, and wanted always to be thus on her. And six or eight times, when the other nun did not want to sleep with her in order to avoid sin, Benedetta went to find her in her bed and, climbing on top, sinned with her by force. Also at that time, during the day, pretending to be sick and showing that she had some need, she grabbed her companion's hand by force, and putting it under herself, she would have her put her finger in her genitals, and holding it there she stirred herself so much that she corrupted herself. And she would kiss her and also by force would put her own hand under her companion and her finger into her genitals and corrupted her. And when the latter would flee, she would do the same with her own hands. Many times she locked her companion in the study, and making her sit down in front of her, by force she put her hands under her and corrupted her; she wanted her companion to do the same to her, and while she was doing this she would kiss her. She always appeared to be in a trance while doing this. Her angel, Splenditello, did these things, appearing as a boy of eight or nine years of age. This angel Splenditello through the mouth and hands of Benedetta, taught her companion to read and write, making her be near her on her knees and kissing her and putting her hands on her breasts. And the first time she made her learn all the letters without forgetting them; the second, to read the whole side of a page; the second day she made her take the small book of the Madonna and read the words; and Benedetta's two other angels listened to the lesson and saw the writing.

This Splenditello called her his beloved; he asked her to swear to be his beloved always and promised that after Benedetta's death he would always be with her and would make himself visible. He said I want you to promise me not to confess these things that we do together, I assure you that there is no sin in it; and while we did these things he said many times: give yourself to me with all your heart and soul and then let me do as I wish. Other times he said that if I were a man and always made new promises.

The same angel managed it so that neither Benedetta nor her companion did the usual [spiritual] exercises that the nuns did prior to general confession. He made the sign of the cross all over his companion's body after having committed many immodest acts with her; [he also said] many words that she couldn't understand and when she asked him why he was doing this, he said that he did this for her own good. Jesus spoke to her companion [through Benedetta] three times, twice before doing these dishonest things. The first time he said he wanted her to be his bride and he was content that she give him her hand; and she did this thinking it was Jesus. The second time it was in the choir at Forty Hours, holding her hands

together and telling her that he forgave her all her sins.
The third time it was after she was disturbed by these
goings on, and he told her that there was no sin involved
whatsoever and that Benedetta while doing these things
had no awareness of them. All these deeds her companion
confessed with very great shame.

Benedetta is the cleanest of all the nuns, so that not
only the nuns but also lay people are astonished since St.
Francis, St. Catherine of Siena, and other saints were
contemptuous of cleanliness. And while she was in ecstasy, her angel excused her on this account, saying that
these other saints also did not have the guardians that
she did.

Notes

Introduction

1. Florence, Archivio di Stato (henceforth ASF), *Miscellanea Medicea*, 376, ins. 28.

2. See, for example, Andrew Marvell's poem, "Upon Appleton House," written in mid-seventeenth century, and Denis Diderot's *La religieuse* (1760s).

3. The sources for contemporary attitudes are summarized in Ian Maclean, *The Renaissance Notion of Woman: A study in the fortunes of scholasticism and medical science in European intellectual life* (Cambridge, 1980).

4. Heinrich Kramer and James Sprenger, *The Malleus Maleficarum*, Part 2, Q. 1, ch. 2. Originally published ca. 1486, the book quickly became the most influential treatise on witchcraft. See also Erik Midelfort, *Witch-hunting in Southwestern Germany, 1562–1684* (Stanford, 1972), pp. 105–6.

5. The fact that in recent years the extensive researches in the European criminal and Inquisitorial archives by scholars such as Carlo Ginzburg, Patricia Labalme, W. E. Monter, and Guido Ruggiero have revealed almost no cases of lesbian sexuality supports the notion that this charge was generally ignored. For Germany there is mention of one girl drowned by the authorities at Speier in 1477 and one trial in 1721. For France, the jurist Jean Papon devotes one paragraph of his book on law to a case brought before

the *parlement* of Toulouse in 1533. Henri Estienne cites another case that came to trial two years later. And Michel Montaigne, in his *Diary of a Journey to Italy*, briefly describes the sad story of a young woman who was hanged in 1580 for engaging in a lesbian affair. For Spain we have Antonio Gomez' report that two nuns were accused of "using material instruments," for which they were burned at the stake. In addition, there are the observations of prison life by Cristobal de Chaves, who noted that some female prisoners "made themselves into roosters" by fashioning penises which they tied to themselves. For Switzerland there exists only one case, which came to trial in 1568, and for the Netherlands, an early seventeenth-century case is cited by the physician Nicolas Tulp. Most of these cases are cited by Louis Crompton to argue that lesbian sexuality was as serious a concern as male homosexuality and that it was punished just as severely. L. Crompton, "The Myth of Lesbian Impunity: Capital Laws from 1270 to 1791," *Journal of Homosexuality*, 6 (Fall/Winter 1980/81): 17; see also E. W. Monter, "La sodomie a l'epoque moderne en Suisse romande," *Annales, E.S.C.*, 29 (July/Aug. 1974): 1029–30; and Mary Elizabeth Perry, *Crime and Society in Early Modern Seville* (Hanover, 1982); L.S.A.M. von Romer, "Der Uranismus in den Niederlanden bis zum 19. Jahrhundert, mit besonderer Berucksichtigung der grossen Uranierverfolgung in Jahre 1730," *Jahrbuch für sexuelle Zwischenstufen*, 8 (1906): 365–512. A more detailed discussion of these trials and their implications can be found elsewhere in the introduction as well as in Chapter 5.

6. St. Ambrose, *Commentarii in omnes Pauli epistolas*, cited in Crompton, "Lesbian Impunity," p. 14. Many of the sources and opinions mentioned in the following few pages have also been cited in four surveys that are fundamental to any work on the subject. Listed in the order in which they were first published, they are Derrick S. Bailey, *Homosexuality and the Western Christian Tradition* (London, 1955; reprinted Hamden, Conn., 1975); Michael Goodich, "Sodomy in Medieval Secular Law," *Journal of Homosexuality*, 1:3 (1976): 295–302; John Boswell, *Christianity, Social Tolerance, and Homosexuality: Gay People in Western Europe from the Beginning of the Christian Era to the Fourteenth Century* (Chicago, 1980), and L. Crompton, "Lesbian Impunity."

7. St. John Chrysostom, *In Epistolam ad Romanos*; the full text

of the fourth homily is translated and reproduced in Boswell, *Social Tolerance and Homosexuality*, pp. 359–62.

8. Cited in Crompton, "Lesbian Impunity," p. 14.

9. Peter Abelard, *Commentarium super S. Pauli epistolam ad Romanos libri quinque*, in J.-P. Migne, ed., *Patrologiae cursus completus: Serie Latinae*, 178, p. 806.

10. Penitential of Theodore of Tarsus, in John McNeill and Helena M. Gammer, eds., *Medieval Handbooks of Penance* (New York, 1938), p. 185; Venerable Bede, "De Remediis peccatorum," in Migne, *Patrologiae Latinae*, 94, pp. 569–70. Penitential of Pope Gregory III, J. D. Mansi, *Sacrorum conciliorum nova et amplissima collectio* (Graz, 1960), 12:293, 295; also cited in Bailey, *Homosexuality*, p. 106.

11. St. Thomas Aquinas, *Summa theologiae*, II.ii.94:11–12.

12. See the rubric *luxuria* in Sylvester Prierias Mazzolini, *Summa summarum, que Sylvestrina dicitur* (Bologna, 1515); Jean Gerson, "De septem vitiis capitalibus," in L. E. Du Pin, *Opera omnia* (Antwerp, 1706), I:345–46.

13. St. Antoninus, *Somma dello arcivescovo Antonio omnis mortalium cura*; St. Charles Borromeo, "Poenitentiale Mediolanense," in F. W. H. Wasserchleben, *Die Büssordnungen der abendlandischen Kirche* (Graz, 1958), pp. 722–23.

14. Letter 211, in St. Augustine, *Letters*, The Fathers of the Church Ser., vol. 32 (New York, 1956).

15. The poem, which is possibly the only example of medieval lesbian literature, was prompted by the temporary absence of one of the lovers. It is addressed "To G., her singular rose, From A.— the bonds of precious love. . . . When I recall the kisses you gave me, And how with tender words you caressed my little breasts, I want to die Because I cannot see you. . . . Come home, sweet love! Prolong your trip no longer; Know that I can bear your absence no longer. Farewell. Remember me." The poem is reproduced in its entirety in Boswell, *Social Tolerance and Homosexuality*, pp. 220–21.

The provisions of the councils of Paris and Rouen are discussed in Bailey, *Homosexuality*, p. 132.

16. Crompton, pp. 15–16.

17. *Ibid.*, p. 18.

18. Cited in Boswell, p. 158.

19. In his brilliant but sometimes controversial book, John Boswell argues that the major turning point in Western attitudes toward homosexuality took place in the thirteenth century, when the treatment of homosexuals became much harsher than before. Much of the concern with homosexuality in legal documents, literature, and elsewhere thus dates from the late medieval period. Most of the sources cited by Boswell in his encyclopedic analysis of the subject do not mention women.

20. St. Peter Damian, *Liber Gomorrhianus*, in Migne, *Patrologiae Latinae*, vol. 145.

21. St. Bernardino of Siena (1380–1444), whose fulminations against male sodomites were legend, may have also preached once or twice against the sodomitical practices of women, but it is not clear what he had in mind. In a sermon preached at Siena in 1427, he states: "They have sinned from birth in many and various ways, as much because of their fathers, who are also sodomites, as because of their mothers, who have a little penchant for evil habits" (p. 902). In another sermon, he commanded that "the husband not depart from the wife.—The husband must not part from the wife, as many do, who are away for three or four or six years, and they leave her unhappy, and sometimes she [. . .]; and you are in lewdness and in sin, and sometimes fall into sodomitical vices, and in many ways you are apt to send both yourself and sometimes her to hell" (p. 402). San Bernardino of Siena, *Le prediche volgari*, P. Bargellini, ed. (Milan, 1936); *Le prediche volgari*, C. Cannarozzi, ed., Sienese sermons, 1425: 2 vols. (Florence, 1958).

22. Dante Alighieri, *The Divine Comedy: Inferno*, Canto 15, transl. John Ciardi (New York, 1982), p. 139.

23. Fiordispina complains about her fate to Love, " 'Tis only I, on earth, in air, or sea, / Who suffer at thy hands such cruel pain; / And this thou hast ordained, that I may be / The first and last example in thy reign. Ludovico Ariosto, *Orlando Furioso*, Canto 25, verse 36.

24. Agnolo Firenzuola, I *Ragionamenti amorosi*, in *Opere*, Delmo Maestri, ed. (Turin, 1977), p. 97; orig. printed in 1548.

25. It is obvious from the tone of Brântome's work that he did not really believe that sexual relations between women had become the height of fashion. He was as eager to spread scandal and engage in malicious gossip as anything else. Nonetheless, the reasons he

gives for either condemning or condoning lesbian practices can be taken to reflect not just personal opinion, but what his audience wanted to believe. Pierre de Bourdeille, Seigneur de Brantôme, *Les Vies des dames galantes* (orig. 17th c., Paris, 1962), pp. 122, 126.

26. *Ibid.*, p. 123.

27. *Ibid.*, p. 126.

28. *Ibid.*, p. 121.

29. St. Augustine, *Contra mendacium*, Cited in Boswell, *Social Tolerance and Homosexuality*, p. 157. Similarly, St. Jerome, for example, brought together well-evolved Greek and Judaic notions when he wrote that "as long as woman is for birth and children, she is different from man as body is from soul. But when she wishes to serve Christ more than the world, then she ceases to be a woman and will be called a man." *Commentarius in Epistolam ad Ephesios*, cited in Vern L. Bullough, "Transvestism in the Middle Ages," Vern L. Bullough and James Brundage, eds., *Sexual Practices and the Medieval Church* (Buffalo, 1982), p. 45.

30. A useful summary of the often conflicting notions of female anatomy and biological role in procreation may be found in Maclean, *Notions of Woman*, pp. 35–38. Also see Steven Greenblatt, "Fiction and Friction," T. Heller, M. Sosna, and D. Wellbery, eds., *Reconstructing Individualism* (Stanford, 1985), forthcoming.

31. Penitential of Theodore, in *Handbooks of Penance*, p. 185.

32. Mansi, *Sacrorum conciliorum*, 12:293, 295, sec. 30.

33. Borromeo, however, gave men only ten to thirty days' penance for self-pollution. *Poenitentiale Mediolanense*, pp. 722–23.

34. "Cil qui sont sodomite prové doivent perdre les c___ [?]. Et se il le fet segond foiz, il doit perdre membre. Et se il le fet la tierce, il doit etre ars. Femme qui le fet doit a chescune foiz perdre membre e la tierce doit estre arsse." This law has been interpreted by scholars in a variety of ways, ranging from loss of testicles, castration, and burning; to castration, loss of a limb, and burning; to loss of a limb and burning. For female sodomites the interpretations offered have included clitorectomies as a possible punishment. See, Bailey, *Homosexuality*, p. 142; Boswell, *Social Tolerance and Homosexuality*, p. 290; and Crompton, "Lesbian Impunity," p. 13.

35. Crompton, "Lesbian Impunity," p. 16.

36. The link between heresy and homosexuality may have

stemmed from the negative attitudes toward procreation held by certain heretical groups such as the Albigensians. Orthodox Christians attributed this horror of insemination to their preference for sodomitical practices. See Arlo Karlen, "The Homosexual Heresy," *Chaucer Review*, 6:1 (1971): 44–63; Vern L. Bullough, "Heresy, Witchcraft, and Sexuality," Vern Bullough and James Brundage, eds., *Sexual Practices and the Medieval Church* (Buffalo, 1982), pp. 206–17.

37. Increased repression of sodomy in the sixteenth century has also been noted by William Monter, *Ritual, Myth and Magic in Early Modern Europe* (Thetford, Norfolk, 1983), pp. 116–17. With respect to Geneva, which he studied in particular detail, Monter sees a clear correlation between sodomy prosecutions and increased religious fervor between 1560–1610. Elsewhere there were also other influences at work. In Spain, for instance, M. E. Perry cites the authorities' desire to consolidate a newly formed political order. *Crime and Society in Seville*, p. 72. Presumably similar pressures were at work in England.

38. Cited in Crompton, "Lesbian impunity," p. 18.

39. *Ibid*.

40. *Las siete partidas del sabio rey Don Alonso el Nono, nuevamente glosadas por el licenciado Gregorio Lopez* (Salamanca 1829–31; reprint of 1565 ed.), vol. 3, p. 178.

41. Antonio Gomez, *Ad leges Tauri*, L. 80, n. 34; the text of this opinion is reproduced in its entirety in *Miss Marianne Woods and Miss Jane Pirie Against Dame Cumming Gordon* (New York, 1975), "Authorities," p. 5. It is also cited in Crompton, "Lesbian Impunity," p. 19.

42. Prospero Farinacci, *De delictics carnis*, Q. 148, T. 16, *Miss Marianne Woods*, p. 4.

43. "De bono conjugali," in St. Augustine, *Treatises on Marriage and Other Subjects*, The Fathers of the Church Ser., vol. 27, pp. 9–51. In the fifteenth century, St. Augustine was frequently cited on the evils of heterosexual sodomy by married couples. The Florentine archbishop, St. Antoninus, for example, went so far as to say: "Saint Augustine tells us that a woman should rather let herself be killed than to consent to such a mortal sin." St. Antoninus, *Somma dello arcivescovo Antonino: Omnis mortalium cura*, p. 80. Somewhat more practical, St. Augustine had actually advised women

to send their husbands to a prostitute rather than to submit. He reasoned that adultery was a less reprehensible sin.

44. St. Augustine, Letter 211.

45. Penitential of Theodore, p. 185.

46. Rubric 21 of his penitential, entitled "On Sodomists," deals with homosexuality among clerics and also among boys. Rubric 30, "On Diverse and Minor Sins," deals with coitus between women (probably mutual) masturbation, and anal intercourse, as well as other nonsexual transgressions. Mansi, *Sacrorum conciliorum*, 12:293, 295. For a different interpretation of these rubrics, see Boswell, *Social Tolerance and Homosexuality*, p. 180.

47. Albertus Magnus, *Summa theologiae*, cited in Boswell, *Social Tolerance and Homosexuality*, pp. 316–18.

48. Thomas Aquinas, *Summa*, II.ii.93 and 94.

49. Antoninus, *Somma*, pp. 77–80.

50. Borromeo, *poenitentiale*, pp. 722–23.

51. Vincent Filluccio, *Moralium quaestionum*, cited in Lodovico Maria Sinistrari, *De sodomia*, item 8. Originally published in Rome in 1700, as part of his larger work, *De delictis et poenis*, Sinistrari's work was published many times thereafter, both in Latin and in vernacular languages.

52. Cited in Sinistari, *De sodomia*, item 39.

53. *Ibid.*, item 1.

54. In this book I have used the terms "lesbian sexuality" and "lesbian nun" for reasons of convenience to describe acts and persons called "lesbian" in our own time. We must be aware, however, of the limitations of these terms and of the fact that for many reasons they were not and could not have been used before the late nineteenth century, when new ways of thinking about women and women's sexuality began to emerge. See George Chauncey, "From Sexual Inversion to Homosexuality: Medicine and the Changing Conceptualization of Female Deviance," *Salmagundi*, 58–59 (Fall 1982–Winter 1983): 115–46.

In applying sexual labels, we must remember that sexual experience, labeling, and self-identification are immensely varied and operate within socially defined categories that influence identity and behavior. Before the nineteenth century, women who engaged in sexual relations with other women were incapable of perceiving themselves as a distinct sexual and social group, and were not seen as such by others. The relegation of women to the private sphere precluded such perceptions because it prevented the formation of homosexual subcultures of the sort that were open, for example, to men. Except in convents or brothels, women's lives and sexual identities were circumscribed by their families and the walls of their household.

Because of the complexity of the problem and its links to issues of sexual definition in the present, in recent years there has been much debate about whether to apply the term "lesbian" to the pre-modern era. Adrienne Rich, for instance, has posited a lesbian continuum, in which lesbian identity is tied not so much to a self-conscious identity or even to sexual relations or attractions, but to emotional bonds that emerge between women in the midst of a patriarchal society. Thus all women in the past who at some point in their lives chafed under the limits imposed on them by men and who felt certain ties of solidarity or kinship with other women might be called lesbian ("Compulsory Heterosexuality and Lesbian Existence," *Signs: Journal of Women in Culture and Society*, 5:4 (Summer 1980): 631–60. The problem with this position is that it is fundamentally ahistorical in its inclusiveness. A different stance is taken by Anne Ferguson who argues that while some women can be described as sexually deviant in that they departed from the norm, the term "lesbian" should not be applied to women who lived before its emergence as a cultural category in the late nineteenth century. ("Patriarchy, Sexual Identity, and the Sexual Revolution," *Signs*, 7:1 (Autumn 1981): 158–66. While I am in agreement with the substance of this argument, for practical reasons of language I have not subscribed to its conclusions.

Similar issues have also come up in recent debates about the use of sexual labels for men. It is important to emphasize, however, that the history of male homosexuality differs from that of women's both with respect to when changes occurred and what social and intellectual currents influenced them. Among the most clearly articulated arguments against employing the category of "homosexual" to periods before the late nineteenth century are those of Jeffrey Weeks in *Coming Out: Homosexual Politics in Britain from the Nineteenth Century to the Present* (London, 1977). This view is shared by Michel Foucault, *The History of Sexuality: An Introduction*, vol. 1

(New York, 1978). Opposing views are held by John Boswell, "Towards the Long View: Revolutions, Universals and Sexual Categories," *Salmagundi*, 58–59 (Fall-Winter 1983): 89–113. Boswell's stance has gained additional support through the findings of Guido Ruggiero that a male homosexual subculture existed in Renaissance Venice, *The Boundaries of Eros: Sex Crime and Sexuality in Renaissance Venice* (Oxford Press, 1985). A useful summary of the controversy as well as a cautious endorsement for further exploration of homosexual subcultures can be found in Stephen Murray and Kent Gerard, "Renaissance Sodomite subcultures?," in *Among Men, Among Women: Sociological and Historical Recognition of Homosocial Arrangements* (Amsterdam, 1983).

55. The rediscovery of Sappho's poetry in mid-sixteenth century did not immediately lead to the adoption of the term "lesbian" for women. Indeed, contemporaries had difficulties accepting the sexual preferences of a poet of such obvious distinction and a few sporadic efforts were made to give them a heterosexual interpretation. Francois Rigolot, "Louise Labé et la redécouverte de Sappho," *Nouvelle revue du seizieme siècle*, 1 (1983): 19–31. Marie-Jo Bonnet, *Un choix sans équivoque: Recherches historiques sur les relations amoureuses entre les femmes, XVI–XXᵉ siècle* (Paris, 1981), pp. 21–67.

56. Sinistrari, *De Sodomia*, item 7.

57. *Ibid.*, items 13, 15–17, 21–22. Reasoning backwards, Sinistrari used as evidence of physiological differences between Western and non-Western women, the allegedly common Middle Eastern practice of performing clitoridectomies on young girls. If the operations were performed, they must have been needed. He also cites several examples of such operations in Europe, one of them involving a nun who nearly lost her life in the process.

58. *Ibid.*, items 29, 50.

59. *Ibid.*, item 23.

60. Lopez, *Las siete partidas*; Jean Gerson, *Confessional ou Directoire des confesseurs*, no date, late fifteenth century. P. Glorieux questions the authorship of this text, but for our purposes what matters is that Renaissance readers attributed it to Gerson. See Jean Gerson, *Opera omnia*, ed. by P. Glorieux (Paris, 1960), I:85.

61. Monter, "La Sodomie," p. 1029.

62. As late as the nineteenth century, legal authorities, for reasons quite different from those of earlier times, refused to believe

that women could engage in sexual relations with each other. Illustrative of nineteenth-century attitudes is the case retold by Lillian Faderman, in *Scotch Verdict* (New York, 1983).

Yet even in our own century, the subject of lesbian sexuality has not received the attention it deserves. Eileen Power's *Medieval English Nunneries* (Cambridge, 1922), for example, does not mention the subject, and neither do more recent and revisionary works on medieval convents, despite their emphasis on the bonds of solidarity and community that existed behind convent walls. As for books on the history of sexuality, general books on the subject have tended to ignore lesbians. Michel Foucault's widely cited works, for instance, make almost no reference to them, and his argument that certain forms of sexuality were denied by Western society only starting in the seventeenth century can only have been made by completely disregarding the treatment of lesbian sexuality in the medieval and early modern period. Turning to more specialized works, the rapidly proliferating literature on male homosexuality has not produced a comparable literature on the history of lesbians or lesbian sexuality. This kind of neglect led Louis Crompton to observe, as recently as 1981: "Little has been written about lesbianism and the law from a historical point of view. Indeed, I am not aware of a single modern essay on the subject." ("Lesbian Impunity," p. 11) His lament can be extended to almost every other aspect of lesbian sexuality in the past. The subject does not yet have a history.

Chapter One: The Family

1. "The holy council anathematizes each and all persons, of whatever character or rank they may be, whether clerics or laics, seculars or regulars, and with whatever dignity invested, who shall, except in the cases permitted by law, in any way force any virgin or widow, or any other woman whatsoever, to enter a monastery against her will, or to take the habit of any religious order or make profession; those also who give advice, aid or encouragement, as well as those who, knowing that she does not enter the monastery or receive the habit, or make profession; those also who give advice, aid or encouragement, as well as those who,

knowing that she does not enter the monastery or receive the habit, or make profession voluntarily, shall in any way take part in that act their presence, consent or authority. Similarly does it anathematize those who shall in any way and without a just cause impede the holy wish of virgins or other women to take the veil or pronounce the vows." *Canons and Decrees of the Council of Trent*, H. J. Schroeder, trans. (St. Louis, 1941), Twenty-fifth Session, ch. 28. The Council also fixed the minimum age of religious profession at sixteen. Presumably at that age a girl was old enough to give a fully mature and free consent. Twenty-fifth Session, ch. 15.

2. Archivio di Stato, Pisa (henceforth ASPi), *Corporazioni Religiose*, 924, S. Domenico di Pescia, ins. 1. Unfortunately, the first section of the diary is missing so we do not know the name of the nun who wrote it.

3. Arcangela Tarabotti's "L'inferno monacale" was left unpublished. Her *Tirannia paterna* was published the year of her death under the title *La semplicità ingannata*. For a discussion and excerpts of both works, see *Donna e società nel Seicento*, Ginevra Conti Odorisio, ed. (Rome, 1979), pp. 199–214.

4. ASF, *Decima Granducale*, 7135, pp. 1–6. In 1602 Giuliano's tax return listed 30 parcels of land valued at 839 scudi. The largest landholder was his father-in-law, Antonio di Piero di Martino Pieri, who owned 45 parcels valued at 1,520 scudi.

5. Giuliano's brother-in-law, Domenico Antonio Pieri, is mentioned in his will, made out on November 7, 1620. ASPi, *Corp. Relig.*, 924, ins. 1.

6. Giuliano left his married sister two *staia* (1.4 bushels) of chestnut flour per year and divided the rest of his estate in equal portions among his mother, wife, and daughter Benedetta. *Ibid.*

7. Cited in James Bruce Ross, "The Middle-Class child in Urban Italy," in Loyd deMause, ed., *The History of Childhood* (New York, 1974), p. 185. Among the truly difficult first tasks of a father, the fifteenth-century humanist Leon Battista Alberti cites that of finding an adequate wet-nurse. Alberti, *The Family in Renaissance Florence*, René Neu Watkins, trans. (Columbia, S.C., 1969), p. 51. Because they were well aware of the dangers of sending infants to wet-nurses, preachers and moralists vociferously upbraided parents for this common practice, which may in some instances, especially in the case of female infants, have been a veiled form of infanticide.

See, among others, Richard C. Trexler, "Infanticide in Florence: New Sources and First Results," in *History of Childhood Quarterly*, 1 (1973): 96–116; Christiane Klapisch-Zuber, "Genitori naturali e genitori di latte," *Quaderni Storici*, 44 (1980): 543–563.

8. Cited in Ross, "The Middle-Class Child," p. 186. When parents hired a wet-nurse they therefore not only bought her services as a provider of food but they contracted for her sexual life as well. Nothing made parents fetch their infants quicker from the house of a wet-nurse than the discovery that she was pregnant. See Klapisch-Zuber, "Genitori di latte."

9. Although in other respects her education seems typical of that of many other religious women of her time, in being taught by her father Benedetta resembled more the handful of learned women humanists of the Renaissance than the average middle-class women of her day. See W. H. Woodward, *Vittorino da Feltre and Other Humanist Educators* (New York, 1963), pp. 247–50; Margaret L. King, "Book-Lined Cells: Women and Humanism in the Early Italian Renaissance," in Patricia H. Labalme, ed., *Beyond their Sex: Learned Women of the European Past* (New York, 1980), pp. 66–90; Paul Oskar Kristeller, "Learned Women of Early Modern Italy: Humanists and University Scholars," *Ibid.*, pp. 91–116; Patricia H. Labalme, "Women's Roles in Early Modern Venice: An Exceptional Case," *ibid.*, pp. 129–52.

10. ASPi, *Corp. Relig.*, 924, ins. 1.

11. See p. 149.

12. The matter-of-fact quality of miracles in fairy tales is discussed by Max Luthi, who contrasts the uses of miracles in fairy tales with those in local legends and saint's lives, where their function is to astonish, instruct, or frighten. Max Luthi, *Once Upon a Time: On the Nature of Fairy Tales* (Bloomington, 1976), pp. 43–46.

13. One of the most famous and amusing tales based on nightingale symbolism is Giovanni Boccaccio's story of how Messer Lizio di Valbona surprised his daughter sleeping with the young Ricciardo Manardi. Under the pretext of wanting to be "lulled to sleep by the nightingale," the girl had received permission to sleep outside on a balcony where her lover could meet her unseen by her parents. Ricciardo climbed up to the balcony, they lay down together, "and for virtually the entire night they had delight and joy of one another, causing the nightingale to sing at frequent inter-

vals." Giovanni Boccaccio, *Decameron*, fifth day, fourth story. See also the well-known Middle English poem *The Owl and the Nightingale*, attributed to Nicholas de Guildford.

14. Testimony of 1 August, 1619.

15. ASF, *Misc. Med*, 376, ins. 28, *Relatione di Benedetta da Vellano, havuta dal A.A.A. Vescovo d'Anglona*.

Chapter Two: The Convent

1. Fernand Braudel, *The Mediterranean and the Mediterranean World in the Age of Philip II* (London, 1972), vol. 1, p. 34.

2. For a detailed account of this transformation, see Judith C. Brown, *In the Shadow of Florence: Provincial Society in Renaissance Pescia* (New York, 1982).

3. *Ibid.*, pp. 42–43; Gigi Salvagnini, *Pescia, una città* (Florence, 1975), p. 93; ASF, *Regio Diritto*, 4898, fol. 313. We can only make a rough estimate of the percentage of the Pesciatine female population in convents since the convents of the town accepted girls like Benedetta who came from the surrounding area.

4. Carlo Stiavelli, *La storia di Pescia nella vita privata dal secolo XIV al XVIII* (Florence, 1903), p. 164.

5. In sixteenth-century Pescia, only citizens could hold public office and citizenship was restricted to individuals whose families had owned land or other fixed property at Pescia for at least fifty years. Brown, *In the Shadow of Florence*, p. 182.

6. ASF, *Regio Diritto*, 4898, fol. 313.

7. For a more extended discussion of the growing cost of dowries in Tuscany, see David Herlihy and Christiane Klapisch-Zuber, *Les Toscans et leurs familles* (Paris, 1978). In 1619, the papal office that regulated life in the convents of Italy wrote to the provost of Pescia that, henceforth, anyone wishing to become a nun at the convent of Santa Chiara must pay a dowry of at least 400 scudi; Archivio Segreto Vaticano, *Vesc. e Reg. Registri: Regista Regularium*, 24, 29 Nov. 1619.

8. At the time there were as yet no Theatine nuns proper. The order that would later be called the Theatine nuns, with which the Pesciatine community would never be formally associated, had already been founded at Naples in the early 1580s by the Venerable

Ursula Benincasa, but they went by the name of Sisters of the Immaculate Conception of the Virgin Mary. During their first decades, they were under the spiritual direction of Gregorio Navarro, Abbot of Francavilla, who shortly before his death turned them over to the Fathers of the Naples Oratory. Finally, in 1633 Pope Urban VIII placed the Sisters of the Immaculate Conception under the care of the Theatine Order, whose constitution the nuns had already adopted. Despite the similarity of aspirations for a reformed church, the Theatine nuns of Naples were in no way related to those of Pescia. The latter were an independent congregation which, according to Pirro Torrigiani, one of their administrators, was comprised of eighteen women whose combined dowries came to 2900 scudi. ASPi, *Corp. Relig.*, 924, ins. 1. On the origins of the Theatine nuns at Naples, see Gaetano Moroni, *Dizionario di erudizione storico-ecclesiastica* (Venice, 1855), vol. 73, pp. 31–109.

9. ASPi, *Corp. Relig*, 924, ins. 1.

10. *Ibid.*

11. The moral condition of Italian convents in the sixteenth century is described by P. Paschini, in "I monasteri femminili in Italia nel Cinquecento," *Problemi di vita religiosa in Italia nel Cinquecento: Atti del convegno di storia della Chiesa in Italia* (Padua, 1960), pp. 31–60.

12. The opening remarks of the edict of 1545, which put many of these provisions into effect, reveal the great concern of Cosimo de' Medici for the well-being of Tuscan convents. The edict is justified on the grounds that "It being the will of our most illustrious and excellent lord, the lord duke of Florence, that the monasteries of nuns of his city and ducal state grow in perfect religion and that they be well kept and governed in both spiritual and temporal affairs, so that concentrating on the contemplative life and on the service of God, their prayers for the preservation and health of His Excellency and of the entire population of the city and dominion will deserve to be heard by his great majesty." ASF, *Magistrato Supremo*, 10, fols. 19v–20v; reprinted in Arnaldo D'Addario, *Aspetti della Controriforma a Firenze* (Rome, 1972), pp. 480–82. D'Addario discusses this and other legislation on pp. 124–43.

13. ASF, *Mediceo del Principato*, 326, fols. 32v–34v, reprinted in *Ibid.*, pp. 484–85.

14. ASF, *Reggio Diritto*, 4898, fols. 222–44, 265.

15. *Ibid.*, fols. 1021–36.

16. The male order of Theatines founded by St. Cajetan grew out of his involvement with the Oratory of Divine Love. St. Cajetan was particularly interested in regenerating the Catholic church from within by reforming the clergy and returning the church to its apostolic simplicity. He therefore created the first order of regular clergy—i.e., clergy who lived according to a common rule. Monks, of course, had lived in this fashion since the early days of the church but by the sixteenth century it became apparent that the most pressing need for reform was in the life of the clergy that ministered to the secular world since they were the most readily visible to the laity. Creating a rule for the governance of clergy's daily life would bring about a higher moral and spiritual standard. This notion was then taken up by the Jesuits, the Barnabites, and all new orders of the sixteenth century.

Although they were not formally associated with the Theatines, the Pesciatine Fathers of the Holy Annunciation shared the same aspirations and some of their founders moved in the reformed circles of the Theatines and other new orders. The similarity of goals and daily practices finally led, in 1623, to the merger of the Pesciatine group with the Barnabites, an order whose austere way of life made them unreceptive to most such mergers.

The histories of some of these reform groups can be found in Pio Paschini, *S. Gaetano Thiene, Gian Pietro Carafa e le origini dei Chierici Regolari Teatini* (Rome, 1926); Paul A. Kunkel, *The Theatines in the History of the Catholic Reform Before the Establishment of Lutheranism*, Ph.D. Diss., Catholic University of America, 1941; "Barnabites," in *The New Catholic Encyclopedia* (New York, 1947), vol. 2, p. 103. On the Fathers of the Holy Annunciation of Pescia, see *Dizionario degli Istituti di Perfezione* (Rome 1973), vol. 6, pp. 1081–82; L. Manzini, *L'apostolato di Pescia: Antonio M. Pagni, fondatore della Congregazione della Santissima Annunziata, barnabita (1556–1623)* (Rome, 1941).

17. The so-called "Rule" of St. Augustine is really a letter the Saint addressed to a group of nuns, led by his sister, who were experiencing difficulties in the governance of their convent. The letter was widely taken up by female communities in the Middle Ages as the basis for their own more specific rules. Saint Augustine, Letter 211, in *The Fathers of the Church*, vol. 32.

18. In 1648, the nuns voted 16 to 1 in favor of a constitution, which then had to be approved by the provost of Pescia. He apparently had no difficulties approving it but balked at their request to be allowed to publish it. To strengthen their argument, in 1652 the nuns wrote to the provost that they had just received the published constitution of the Nuns of the Annunciation of Genoa. They pointed out that in the 39 years since their foundation and the publication of their constitution in 1643, that group had founded 43 new monasteries. This, they argued, was obvious proof that published rules did not keep girls from joining convents. Faced with such irrefutable logic, the provost capitulated and Giovanni Martellini, the nuns' father confessor was given permission to go ahead with the project. ASPi, *Corp. Relig.*, ins. 1.

19. *Ibid.*

20. *Ibid.*

21. A detailed picture of the congregation's financial situation is impossible to obtain since no account books survive and our only sources are written summaries sent to Rome as part of their application to become a regular convent. It appears from these sources that the group's annual revenues came to 300 scudi, of which half came from the silk work done by its members. In addition, the congregation obtained unspecified amounts of grain, wine, and olive oil from the dowries paid in kind by some of the girls. According to one report, "with their dowries and with the earnings from their work, in the year 1610 they bought a farm in the commune of Fucecchio for 1750 scudi." The report goes on to state that they had no other sources of income. ASPi, *Corp. Relig.*, 924, ins. 1.

22. *Ibid.*

23. "The holy council . . . commands all bishops that . . . they make it their special care that in all monasteries subject to them by their own authority and in others by the authority of the Apostolic See, the enclosure of nuns be restored wherever it has been violated and that it be preserved where it has not been violated; restraining with ecclesiastical censures and other penalties, every appeal being set aside, the disobedient and gainsayers, even summoning for this purpose, if need be, the aid of the secular arm. The holy council exhorts all Christian princes to furnish this aid, and binds thereto under penalty of excommunication to be incurred

ipso facto all civil magistrates. No nun shall after her profession be permitted to go out of the monastery, even for a brief period under any pretext whatever, except for a lawful reason to be approved by the bishop; any indults and privileges whatsoever notwithstanding. Neither shall anyone, of whatever birth or condition, sex or age, be permitted, under penalty of excommunication to be in curred *ipso facto* to enter the enclosure of a monastery without the written permission of the bishop or the superior." *Canons and Decrees of the Council of Trent*, Session 25, ch. 5.

24. ASPi, *Corp. Relig.*, 924, ins. 1; Biblioteca Capitolare di Pescia, *Visita Falconcini*, fols. 555r–555v.

25. According to the decrees of the Council of Trent, abbesses could be less than forty years old only if there were no nuns in the convent who were older and who had lived commendable monastic lives for at least eight years. Since the Congregation of the Mother of God had several such nuns in its midst, the selection of Benedetta is all the more unusual. *Canons and Decrees of the Council of Trent*, Session 25, ch. 7; ASPi, *Corp. Relig.*, 924, ins. 1.

In part, the choice of Benedetta as abbess may have been related to her literacy and administrative capabilities. As evidence of these we have extant one letter that she wrote to Rome in September 1620 regarding the nomination of four temporal administrators for the convent. The letter was in response to a request by the Vicar of Pescia to submit a list of roughly eight suitable candidates. Benedetta submitted the list and pointed out her four favorites along with her reasons for doing so. The men she suggested were all "of mature age, benefactors of the convent, and well disposed to it." Her letter is well written and straightforward. ASF, *Regio Diritto*, 4898, fol. 1009.

Chapter Three: The Nun

1. The didactic purpose of saints' legends and their relationship to literate, official culture is discussed in Luthi, *Once Upon a Time* (Bloomington, 1976), pp. 37–46; see also Hippolyte Delehaye, *The Legends of the Saints* (New York, 1962; orig. 1905), pp. 3–85; Peter Brown, *The Cult of the Saints: Its Rise and Function in Late Antiquity*

(Chicago, 1981); A. Vauchez, *La saintété en Occident aux derniers siècles du Moyen Age* (Rome, 1981).

2. Testimony of Margherita Ricordati, 23 July, 1619; Testimony of Benedetta Carlini, 1 August, 1619.

3. Testimony of 8 July, 1619.

4. Testimony of 4 July, 1619.

5. *Ibid.*

6. *The Garden of Prayer* (Venice 1494), cited in Michael Baxandall, *Painting and Experience in Fifteenth Century Italy* (Oxford, 1972) p. 46; also Luis de Granada, *Manuale di orationi et spirituali esercitii. Aggionta una breve instruttione per coloro che cominciano a servire Dio dal medesimo autore* (Venice, 1568). Charles Borromeo, *Ammaestramenti di San Carlo Borromeo alle persone religiose*, 2nd. ed. (Milan, 1902).

7. Testimony of 4 July, 1619.

8. Baxandall, *Painting and Experience*, pp. 45–47. Numerous fifteenth and sixteenth century treatises on the correct depiction of religious images in art testify to the importance attached to visual images for the enhancement of prayer and for teaching a still largely illiterate audience. One example from Benedetta's own time is Federico Borromeo's *De pictura sacra*, published in Milan in 1624. The modern edition of this work was edited by Carlo Castiglioni (Sora, 1932).

9. Testimony of 10 July, 1619.

10. Since the boundaries separating religious from secular imagery were not very firm, it may well be that the garden in Benedetta's visions was also derived from the garden of love in secular painting. Although this theme had gone into decline in Tuscan art of the sixteenth century, it had been a popular motif a century earlier, when it was commonly adopted for household decoration and in utensils and furniture associated with marriage and birth ceremonies. For a fuller discussion, see Paul Watson, *The Garden of Love in Tuscan Art of the Early Renaissance* (Philadelphia, 1979).

11. St. Athanasius (c. 296–373) was among the first writers to explore in detail how demons attack human beings, especially monks. Because the devil had an aversion to virtue and piety, he was particularly attracted to monks and felt doubly proud when he managed to ensnare one of them. The fear that this might happen to them remained a constant in the writings of medieval and early modern mystics. St. Teresa of Avila, the sixteenth-century mystic

whose life and works were powerful influences on the female
religious communities of her time, mirrored this concern. When
she began to experience the first stages of mystical transport in
prayer, she "began to be afraid . . . and [I] would begin to wonder
if it was the devil who wanted me to believe it was a good thing,
so that he might deprive me of my mental prayer, and prevent me
from thinking about the Passion and making use of my understanding." See St. Athanasius of Alexandria, *Life of St. Anthony*,
trans. and edited by A. Robertson in *A Select Library of Nicene and
Post-Nicene Fathers*, ed. by P. Schaff and H. Wace, vol. 4 (New York,
1892), pp. 202–3; St. Teresa of Jesus [Avila], *The Life*, in *The Complete
Works of St. Teresa*, trans. and edited by E. Allison Peers (London,
1963), p. 145.

12. Testimony of 4 and 8 July, 1619.

13. *Ibid*.

14. Saint Athanasius, *The Life of St. Anthony*, pp. 205–6. St. Thomas
Aquinas and other theologians took up this idea in later centuries
and it became a common theme in the literature on mysticism.
Joan of Arc, St. Catherine, and St. Theresa, among others, validated
their visions through the emotional states they produced.

15. Testimony of 4 July, 1619.

16. The Bible itself acknowledged the legitimacy of personal revelations and other divine gifts like visions: "Now there are divers-
ities of gifts, but the same Spirit," wrote St. Paul, "For to one is
given by the Spirit the word of wisdom; to another the word of
knowledge by the same Spirit; to another faith by the same Spirit;
to another the gifts of healing by the same Spirit; to another the
working of miracles; to another prophecy; to another discerning of
spirits; to another divers kinds of tongues; to another the interpretation of tongues." [1 Cor. 12:8–10].

17. The repression of apparitions starting in the early sixteenth
century is discussed by William A. Christian, Jr., in *Apparitions in
Late Medieval and Renaissance Spain* (Princeton, 1981), pp. 150–87. In
1516 the Fifth Lateran Council ruled that "supposed apparitions
before they are made public or preached to the people, should be
considered from now on reserved for the examination of the Apostolic seat. If this causes undue delay, or if some urgent need
counsels other action, then the matter should be brought to the
local bishop," cited in *Ibid*., p. 151. This attempt to regain control

over all aspects of Christian life was reinforced in mid-sixteenth century by the Council of Trent's decree that "no new miracles be accepted and no relics recognized unless they have been investigated and approved by the same bishop, who as soon as he has obtained any knowledge of such matters, shall, after consulting theologians and other pious men, act thereon as he shall judge consonant with truth and piety." *Canons and Decrees of the Council of Trent*, Session 25, "On the Invocation, Veneration, and Relics of Saints, and on Sacred Images."

18. Jean Gerson, *De examinatione doctrinarum*, pt. 1, considerations 2a and 3a, in Glorieux, ed. *Oeuvres*, vol. 9.

19. The Petrine image of the weaker vessel [1 Peter 3:7] recurs not only in the writings of men, but of women as well. St. Theresa, for example, refers to "poor women like myself, who are weak and lack fortitude," *The Life*, p. 68. Undoubtedly, there was more than a touch of self-conscious irony in her use of this language, but this in itself reveals the pervasiveness of the image among her male and female audience.

20. Ian Maclean, *The Renaissance Notion of Woman* (Cambridge, 1980), p. 21.

21. Testimony of 8 July, 1619.

22. Female saints were much more prone than men to suffer incapacitating illnesses. Some of these were brought on by the extreme asceticism to which female saints were inclined, but others resulted from their strong desires to deny their corporal needs and existence. Although this may have been a form of self-hatred and self-abasement, contemporaries viewed their fortitude in dealing with their infirmities as a sign of their holiness. For a fuller discussion of the penitential activities of female saints, see, Donald Weinstein and Rudolph M. Bell, *Saints and Society* (Chicago, 1982), pp. 220–38.

23. Summary of Testimony, undated.

24. Testimony of 10 July, 1619.

25. Because in the long run she was unable to repress her conflict fully, and eventually exhibited other types of personality disorders, Benedetta probably did not experience a complete conversion reaction. Nonetheless, her conversion-like symptoms are generally in keeping with conversion reaction, first described by Josef Breuer and Sigmund Freud in the 1890s. The psychological phe-

nomena they wrote about involved the conversion of an unresolved psychological conflict into somatic symptoms. Since then, this has been one of the most widely observed and agreed upon psychological phenomena, despite the often noted divisions in the field of psychiatry and the changing interpretations of mental disorders. Admittedly, the diagnostic label used to describe this reaction and the treatments suggested for it have varied as have the social and cultural factors that made it more prevalent in the European society of Freud's time than at others, nonetheless it has been noted in a diverse number of cultural contexts and times as well as in individuals exhibiting different types of character disorders. The symptoms, which usually appear suddenly in adolescence or early adulthood, can vary widely in type and severity, from muscle weakness to paralysis, from difficulties in visual focus to blindness, from mild gastrointestinal symptoms to severe difficulties in swallowing. Yet, underlying the variety of somatic symptoms, the mechanism that accounts for them is the individual's need to blot out a conscious awareness of internal conflicts. It is, at least at some levels, a successful defense mechanism for dealing with anxiety in that it allows the individual to repress the source of conflict and to express it in a symbolic way that is either a representation or a partial solution to the conflict. In addition, the onset of illness may either enable the person to avoid engaging in the activity that may have been the source of conflict or might make others more attentive, thus giving them the support, the love, and the care they might otherwise lack. For this reason, as the anthropologist I. M. Lewis has noted, ailments attributed to possession, whether demoniacal or other, appear frequently among the oppressed groups in a society, particularly women. Denied a more direct way of obtaining their goals, illness offers such individuals an indirect method of achieving their aims. It protects them from the expectations of their social superiors while at the same time it allows them to manipulate them. See Ioan M. Lewis, *Ecstatic Religion: An Anthropological Study of Spirit Possession and Shamanism* (Harmondsworth, Eng., 1971), pp. 66–99; also, the "Case of Anna O.," and "Hysterical Conversion," in J. Breuer and S. Freud, *Studies on hysteria*, in *Standard Edition*, 2 (London, 1955), pp. 21–47, 203–14; S. Freud, "Fragment of an analysis of a case of hysteria," *Standard Edition*, 7 (1953): 3–122; L. Rangell, "The nature of conversion," *Journal of the American Psychoanalytic Association*, 7 (1959): 632–62; and, more recently, *Anna O.: Fourteen Contemporary Reinterpretations* (New York, 1983).

26. Testimony of 1 August, 1619, and 8 July, 1619.

27. See, for example, testimony of 15 July, 1619; testimony of Felice di Giovanni Domenico Guerrini, 23 July, 1619.

28. *Abstratto del processo di Benedetta Carlini*, "Delle visioni e estasi." A detailed description of the St. Dorothy's day procession can be found in a letter by Bastiano Galeotti to Captain Domenico Galeotti, 9 February 1550, printed in Carlo Stiavelli, *La storia di Pescia nella vita privata dal secolo XIV al XVIII* (Florence, 1903), p. 197. Flowers were an important part of the cult of St. Dorothy because she was believed to have miraculously produced a basket of roses and apples in response to a mocker's request as she was led to her execution.

29. The importance and meaning of processions in Renaissance cities is discussed in Edward Muir, *Civic Ritual in Renaissance Venice* (Princeton, 1981), and Richard Trexler, *Public Life in Renaissance Florence* (New York, 1980). At Pescia, processions were serious matters as can be seen in the frequency with which the proper order of the participants and the processional route to be followed were discussed in communal deliberations, especially during times of crisis such as the outbreak of plague. The importance of processions can be seen as well as in the town's willingness to appeal to the highest political authority, the grand duke, in case of irreconcilable differences about them. See, for example, the appeal of 1572, ASF, *Pratica Segreta*, 9, ins. 44 and the elaborate procession that accompanied the transfer of the miraculous image of Mary to the Church of Saints Peter and Paul. E. Nucci, *La Madonna di Piè di Piazza* (Pescia, 1936), p. 14.

30. The Virgin's shrine on the bridge became so popular that it created serious traffic congestion on Pescia's most important artery. As a result, plans began to be made in the 1590s to move it to another location but strong jurisdictional disputes arose as almost every church in town felt it had the best claim to the valuable Virgin. In 1601, amid much pomp and ringing of bells, the image was moved to a newly constructed outdoor chapel on the Piazza Ducci next to the bridge, and finally in 1605, after special pleas were made to the grand duke, it was moved to the church of the

Madonna at the Foot of the Piazza. Details of the processions held in each move as well as the communal deliberations and the correspondence of the ecclesiastical and civil authorities on this subject can be found in Gigi Salvagnini, *La Madonna di Pescia dal ponte a pie' di piazza* (Florence, 1977); also, J. Brown, *In the Shadow of Florence*, pp. 120–21.

31. William A. Christian, Jr., *Apparitions*, pp. 187, 194.

32. ASF, *Misc. Med.* 376:28, "Account of the visit made to the Theatine Nuns, alias Holy Mary of Pescia."

33. Testimony of Bartolomea Crivelli, 1 August, 1619. The importance attached to visible signs can also be seen in the case of another seventeenth-century mystic, Angela Mellini. See Luisa Ciammitti, "Una santa di meno: Storia di Angela Mellini, Cucitrice Bolognese (1667–17)," *Quaderni Storici*, 41 (1979): 612.

34. 1 Cor. 14:33–35. Much has been written about St. Paul's statements regarding women. Their meaning is often far from clear. What are we to make, for example, of "Every man praying or prophesying, having his head covered, dishonoureth his head. But every woman that prayeth or prophesieth with her head uncovered dishonoureth her head: for that is even all one as if she were shaven. For if the woman be not covered let her also be shorn: but if it be a shame for a woman to be shorn or shaven, let her be covered."? [1 Cor. 11:4–6] It may well be, as some recent scholarship suggests, that St. Paul did not really believe there was a theological justification for limiting the role of women in the church. Indeed, women were prominent in Paul's own missionary efforts as teachers, evangelists, and leaders of religious communities. On the other hand, in this as in other issues such as taxation, slavery, and so on, Paul was willing to endorse existing social arrangements in order to heal divisions in his fledgling sect. Paul's distinction between the spiritual and the social realms, however, was not maintained by his followers and over the next few centuries theologians interpreted his pronouncements in such a way as to justify the increased subjection of women, both within and outside the church, on religious grounds. Wayne A. Meeks, *The First Urban Christians: The Social World of the Apostle Paul* (New Haven, 1983), pp. 70–71, 81; Elisabeth Schüssler Fiorenza, *In Memory of Her: A Feminist Theological Reconstruction of Christian Origins* (New York, 1983).

35. In Aristotle's account of human generation, women are incomplete and imperfect males: "Just as it sometimes happens that deformed offspring are produced by deformed parents, and sometimes not, so the offspring produced by a female are sometimes female, sometimes not, but male. The reason is that the female is as it were a deformed male; and the menstrual discharge is semen, though . . . it lacks one constituent, and one only, the principle of Soul. . . . Thus the physical part, the body, comes from the female, and the Soul from the male, since the Soul is the essence of a particular body." *De generatione animalium*, II.3. 737a, 738b, trans. by A. L. Peck (Cambridge, Mass., 1943); also, "females are weaker and colder in their nature, and we should look upon the female state as being as it were a deformity, though one which occurs in the ordinary course of nature." *Ibid.*, IV.6. 775a. In the thirteenth century St. Thomas Aquinas modified this notion to accord with the Genesis version of creation and the Christian notion of the equality of souls, but still, the idea of a woman's inferiority remained: "For the Philosopher [Aristotle] says that the female is an incomplete version of the male. But nothing incomplete or defective should have been produced in the first establishment of things. . . . Only as regards nature *in the individual* is woman something defective and incomplete. For the active power of the seed of the male tends to produce something like itself, perfect in masculinity; but the procreation of a female is the result either of the debility of the active power, or of some unsuitability of the material, or of some change effected by external influences. . . . But with reference to nature in the species as a whole, the female is not something incomplete but is according to the plan of nature and is directed to the work of procreation." Thomas Aquinas, *Summa theologiae*, 1a.92, I, italics mine.

36. Tertullian, *Disciplinary, Moral and Ascetical Works* (New York, 1959), cited in Marina Warner, *Alone of all her Sex: The Myth and the Cult of the Virgin Mary* (New York, 1983), p. 58.

37. Francesco Barbaro (1390–1454), "On Wifely Duties," in B. Kohl and R. Witt, eds., *The Earthly Republic: Italian Humanists on Government and Society* (Philadelphia, 1978), p. 206; the prohibitions on the preaching or teaching of women elaborated by medieval theologians are discussed in Vern L. Bullough, "Medieval Medical and Scientific Views of Women," *Viator*, 4 (1973): 487–93; and Eleanor

McLaughlin, "Equality of Souls, Inequality of Sexes: Women in Medieval Theology," in *Religion and Sexism*, ed. by. R. Ruether (New York, 1974), pp. 213–66.

38. Peter Martyr Vermigli, *Loci communes, IV.I*, pp. 588–89 (Heidelberg, 1622), cited in Maclean, *Renaissance Notion of Woman*, p. 21 Discussiono of the limitations on women and the ways in which some of them managed to circumvent them can be found in William A. Christian, Jr., *Apparitions*, and *idem.*, *Local Religion in Sixteenth-Century Spain* (Princeton, 1981); Natalie Zemon Davis, "Women on Top," in her *Society and Culture in Early Modern France* (Stanford, 1975).

39. At about the same time that Benedetta was preaching in Pescia, the visionary Sister Maria Angiola Gini (d. 1664) was allowed to preach in the convent of S. Matteo ad Arcetri just outside of Florence. She eventually gained a large following and influenced a lot of people. See Viviani della Robbia, *Nei Monasteri Fiorentini*, pp. 89–91.

40. *Abstratto del processo di Benedetta Carlini.*

41. Testimony of 10 July, 1969; Testimony of Bartolomea Crivelli, 1 August, 1619.

42. Testimony of Bartolomea Crivelli, 1 August, 1619.

43. Testimony of 10 July, 1619; Testimony of Bartolomea Crivelli, 1 August, 1619.

44. Romances containing the theme of the exchange of hearts, such as King Rene's *Book of Love* [*Le livre du cueur d'amours espris*] had become widespread among the aristocratic circles of northern Italy and the theme appears in a variety of literary contexts.

45. Raymond of Capua, *Life of St. Catherine of Siena*, trans. by G. Lamb (1960); Johannes Jorgensen, *St. Catherine of Siena* (New York, 1938); fra Serafino Razzi, *Vita della venerabile madre suor santa Suor Caterina de' Ricci* (Lucca, 1594), ed. G. di Agresti (Florence, 1965). A variation of the exchange of hearts motif was the taking of the mystic's heart from her body, to be replaced by the instruments of his Passion; see, for example, Ciammitti, "Una santa di meno," p. 612. The principal features of female spirituality and female images of God in the High Middle Ages are discussed in Caroline Walker Bynum, *Jesus as Mother: Studies in the Spirituality of the High Middle Ages* (Berkeley, 1982); and Michael Goodrich, "The Contours of Female Piety in Later Medieval Hagiography," *Church*

History, 50 (1981). Among other things, Bynum stresses the power conferred by men and women to females who had mystical experiences as a result of eucharistic devotions. *Idem*, "Women mystics and eucharistic devotion in the thirteenth century," *Women's Studies*, 11:1–2 (1984): 179–214. Devotion to the Sacred Heart was promoted in the seventeenth century by St. Margaret Mary Alacoque, who was charged by Christ to promote the cult. Auguste Hamon, *Histoire de la devotion au sacre coeur* (Paris 1923–39), 5 vols.

46. Benedetta's spirituality, like that of other women since the late Middle Ages, focused on Christ, the man, rather than the infant or child. Moreover, the Virgin Mary, who loomed so large in the devotion of male clerics, makes only occasional appearances in her visions after she reached adulthood. For an analysis of the male attraction to female religious images and the female attraction to male images, see Simon Roisin's *L'Hagiographie Cistercienne dans le diocese de Liege au XIIIe siècle* (Louvain, 1947).

47. Testimony of 4 July, 1619.

48. Weinstein and Bell, *Saints and Society*, pp. 233–35.

49. Although it is tempting to call Benedetta's fasting anorexia, we need to be extremely cautious in applying such labels to a premodern context. Undoubtedly, Benedetta resembled anorexics in some ways. Like many of them, she was described as a "model child." Similarly, her sudden rejection of food occurred while she was still young and troubled about working out her place in the religious world she inhabited. Furthermore, she exhibited other kinds of compulsive behavior, most notably frequent hand and body washing, which is commonly found in anorexia. On the other hand, she was never described as emaciated and probably did not curtail her eating to the point of endangering her health. [In the rapidly proliferating literature on the subject, see among others, P. Darby, *Anorexia Nervosa: Recent Developments and Research* (New York, 1981) and P. Neuman, *Anorexia and Bulimia* (New York, 1983)] In addition, there are significant social and cultural differences that need to be kept in mind, as Caroline Bynum has pointed out in her work on the function and meaning of food in the spirituality of medieval women. Bynum argues that the fasting of pious women in late medieval and early modern Europe cannot be equated in any simple sense with the food disorders commonly found among young women in modern times. When the specter of famine was

never far away, food had a necessarily different social and religious function than in the modern Western world. Moreover, because both women and Christ, the redeemer, were associated with flesh and food, the latter had a religious significance that it lacks today. Caroline Walker Bynum, "Holy Feast and Holy Fast: Food and Voluntary Starvation in the Piety of Medieval Women," *Representations*, 11 (in press). A different approach is taken by Rudolph Bell, who calls the fasting of medieval female mystics "holy anorexia," thus drawing attention both to the religious and the psychological component of the phenomenon. Whereas modern anorexics strive for perfection in attaining society's ideal of physical beauty, the holy anorexic strives to become more beautiful in the eyes of God. According to Bell, the attempt to attain these kinds of beauty is made through food because in late medieval as in modern times food has been one of the few resources over which women have had control. Food-related behavior has been a way of stressing power, both over their own bodies and over their social environments since it inevitably affects the lives of their families and, in premodern times, even the behavior of religious and political authorities. Rudolph Bell, "Female Piety and Anorexia in Renaissance Tuscany," paper presented at the Conference on Milan and Florence, Villa I Tatti (Florence, 1984); also *idem, Holy anorexia* (Chicago, in press).

50. Theologians such as Albert the Great and writers of medical treatises such as Hildegard of Bingen noted the connection between fasting and amenorrhea. See *Ibid*. Benedetta's concern with cleanliness and the reaction of the other nuns to it is reported in the *Abstratto del Processo di Benedetta Carlini*.

51. A notable Italian example of this type from Benedetta's time is Guido Reni's Madonna of the Rosary. Also see Erwin Panofsky's discussion of the Rosenkrantz Madonna, in *Albert Durer*, vol. 1 (Princeton, 1943).

52. Testimony of 4 July, 1619.

53. Testimony of 12 July, 1619.

54. *Ibid*.

55. Testimony of Bartolomea Crivelli, 23 July, 1619.

56. Testimony of Felice Guerrini, 23 July, 1619.

57. The following description of the events of the day is based on Benedetta's testimony of 12 July, 1619, and that of Felice Guer-

rini, Bartolomea Crivelli, and Margherita Ricordati, 23 July, 1619.

58. E. Allison Peers, *Studies of the Spanish Mystics* (London, 1927–30), 2 vols.; W. Christian, *Apparitions in Spain*, p. 197.

Chapter Four: The First Investigation

1. A brief history of the Cecchi family as well as information on Stefano Cecchi can be found in Michele Cecchi and Enrico Coturri, *Pescia ed il suo territorio nella storia, nell'arte e nelle famiglie* (Pistoia, 1961), pp. 222–31, 338. Some of the negotiations regarding the provostship of Pescia in 1601 can be found in ASF, *Miscellanea Medicea* 348, fols. 720–22.

2. ASF, *Miscellanea Medicea* 376, ins. 28. *Copia: Relatione di Benedetta da Vellano. Havuta dal A. A. A. Vescovo d'Anglona*. Also Testimony of 27 May, 1619.

3. Testimony of 7 June, 1619.

4. Testimony of 15 July, 1619.

5. "I'll tell you what to say and I'll be the one that speaks, not you." Untitled and undated report in *Misc. Med.* 376, ins. 28.

6. Testimony of 15 July, 1619.

7. "I wanted to test what her superiors said about her and I didn't want to say anything." *Ibid.* Benedetta was not the only visionary to write letters while in a trance. The Florentine saint, Maria Maddalena de' Pazzi (1566–1607), occasionally wrote letters to the Pope and other important ecclesiastical officials recommending various steps to reform the Church. In Maria Maddalena's case, however, the letters were never forwarded by her superiors. D'Addario, *Aspetti della Controriforma*, pp. 425–26.

8. Testimony of 14 June, 1619.

9. Testimony of 1 August, 1619.

10. The devastating effects of the plague in Tuscany as well as contemporary perceptions and treatment of it in the early seventeenth century can be found in Carlo M. Cipolla, *Cristofano and the Plague: A Study in the History of Public Health in the Age of Galileo* (Berkeley, 1973); and *Public Health and the Medical Profession in the Renaissance* (New York, 1976).

11. The Appendix contains large portions of the testimony so

that the reader can compare the written record with my recreation of the line of inquiry.

12. The most widely used manual was probably Jean Gerson's *De distinctione verarum revelationum a falsis*; Glorieux, ed., *Oeuvres*, vol. 3, pp. 36–56.

13. The set of questions asked about the stigmata are among the few recorded in the surviving documents.

14. St. Teresa, "The Life," pp. 71, 73.

15. Testimony of 4 July, 1619.

16. *Ibid.*

17. Gerson, "De distinctione," p. 37.

18. St. Teresa, "Spiritual Relations Addressed by Saint Teresa of Jesus to her Confessors," in *The Complete Works*, vol. 1, p. 327.

19. Thomas Aquinas, *Summa theologiae*, 2a.2ae.174, 1 and 2a.2ae.175, 3.

20. St. Teresa, "Interior Castle," ch. 3 and "Life," ch. 20, in *The Complete Works*.

21. St. Teresa, "Life," ch. 18.

22. *Ibid.*, ch. 20.

23. Testimony of 8 July, 1619.

24. *Ibid.*

25. *Ibid.*

26. This ranking may at first glance appear to be the reverse of what it should be, but St. Thomas, as always, had good reason for adopting it. He argues, "Now it is clear that a manifestation of divine truth which derives from a bare contemplation of the truth itself is more effective than that which derives from images of bodily things. Sheer contemplation is in fact nearer to the vision of heaven, according to which truth is gazed upon in the essence of God.

"So it follows that a prophecy which enables some supernatural truth to be perceived, starkly, in terms of intellective vision, is more to be prized than that in which supernatural truth is manifested by likenesses of bodily things in terms of imaginative vision.

". . . the more an agent can attain his end with means which are fewer and better to hand, the more appears to be his capability. Thus a doctor is the more praised when he can heal a sick person by fewer and gentler means.

"Now imaginative vision in prophetic knowledge is not required for its own sake, but for the manifestation of intellectual truth. So all the more effective is prophecy when it has less need of imaginative vision." *Summa theologiae*, 2a.2ae.174.2.

27. Gerson, "De distinctione," pp. 46–47.

28. Testimony of 9 August, 1619. Similarly, on 12 July Benedetta reported that the Virgin told her that she should never be tempted to act against the wishes of her superiors. When questioned during the next interrogation about what the Virgin meant, she answered that "if she had felt any repugnance towards her superiors it would be the same as having felt it against God, having herself experienced that when she had something against them, she did not act well, and she resolved never to raise her eyes against their wishes."

29. Testimony of 8 July, 1619. Ecclesiastical concern with "vain observances of times and hours" and the use of liturgical objects "to ends other than those instituted by the Holy Church" is discussed by Mary R. O'Neil, "Discerning Superstition: Popular Errors and Orthodox Response in Late Sixteenth Century Italy," Ph.D. diss. (Stanford University, 1982), pp. 167–223.

30. Testimony of 12 July, 1619.

31. Testimony of 15 July, 1619.

32. Humility, according to Gerson, is the first and most important virtue of a visionary. Citing various examples from scripture, he argued that the Apostles and the Virgin Mary did not take pride in the visions and other gifts they received from God, but were humbled by them. Rather than brag about what they had seen, they disclosed divine revelations only for the benefit of others or in obedience to divine commandments. Gerson, "De Distinctione," pp. 39–40. St. Teresa also discussses the effects produced by true visions: "The benefits that it [the soul] receives are more numerous and sublime than any which proceed from the previous states of prayer; and its humility is also greater, for it clearly sees how by no efforts of its own it could either gain or keep so exceeding and so great a favour. It also sees clearly how extremely unworthy it is. . . . It sees its own wretchedness. So far is vainglory from it that it cannot believe it could ever be guilty of such a thing. For now it sees with its own eyes that of itself it can do little or nothing, and that it hardly even gave its consent to what has happened to it, but that, against its own will, the door seemed to be closed

upon all the senses so that it might have the greater fruition of the Lord." St. Teresa, "Life," p. 112.

33. Testimony of 8 July, 1619.

34. Testimony of 12 July, 1619.

35. Testimony of 4 July, 1619.

36. Undated, untitled folio.

37. Testimony of 15 July, 1619.

38. ASF, *Regio Diritto*, 4892, fol. 81r.

39. The problems created by the clash of institutional pressures, social class, age, and personalities are revealed nowhere more clearly than in the case of the nun of Monza, immortalized in the nineteenth century by Alessandro Manzoni's *The Betrothed*. In 1607, Sister Virginia Maria de Leyva, the powerful daughter of a Lombard noble family, was brought to trial for conspiring to murder several nuns. Known within her convent as La Signora, she was treated with all the deference and material comforts due to someone of her social standing. Because of her status, she was able to maintain a long-term relationship with a lover, Gianpaolo Osio, with whom she had a child. After several years, however, a young servant girl, in retaliation for a wrong done to her, threatened to tell the authorities, whereupon Sister Virginia had her locked up within the convent and killed by her lover. Despite this preventive measure, her conduct came to the notice of the authorities, who began an investigation. Fearful because of their own involvement in Sister Virginia's affair and the murder of the servant, two of the convent's nuns escaped with the aid of Gianpaolo. Once out, however, one of them was beaten so savagely by her would-be-savior to keep her from talking that she eventually died. The other was seriously hurt when she was thrown down an empty well, stoned, and left for dead. The original court records of the case can be found in C. T. Dandolo, ed., *La Signora di Monza e le streghe del Tirolo: Processi famosi del secolo decimosettimo* (Milan, 1855).

40. The intervention of secular and ecclesiastical authorities in the affairs of Tuscan convents is touched on by D'Addario, *Aspetti della Controriforma*, pp. 113–14. In the neighboring state of Lucca, the misconduct and internal divisions among the nuns of San Giovannetto in the early sixteenth century led the youths of certain noble families to take the law into their own hands.

The civil authorities quickly perceived the threat to public order and jailed many of them for a brief period. See Marino Berengo, *Nobili e mercanti nella Lucca del Cinquecento* (Turin, 1965), pp. 364 ff.

41. Testimony of Bartolomea Crivelli, 23 July, 1619.

42. Testimony of Felice Guerrini, 23 July, 1619.

43. A less strident appeal for public acknowledgment, according to Bartolomea Crivelli, took place at the mystical marriage, when Jesus said through Benedetta that he did not want her to hide her wounds but wanted them to be known, adding that she would not be believed the first, nor the second, nor the third time. Testimony of Bartolomea Crivelli, 23 July, 1619.

44. Testimony of 12 July, 1619.

45. Testimony of 23 July, 1619.

46. Testimony of Margherita Ricordati, 23 July, 1619.

47. *Ibid.*

48. *Ibid.*

49. Testimony of 1 August, 1619.

50. Benedetta described what she saw in her trance during her testimony of 10 July, 1619. The account of the other witnesses dates to 1 August, 1619.

51. This and subsequent statements by Bartolomea regarding the exchange of hearts and the stigmata are part of her testimony of 1 August, 1619.

52. Testimony of 9 and 12 August, 1619.

53. Undated, untitled folios.

54. St. Teresa, "Life," p. 78.

55. Testimony of 23 July, 1619.

56. The Venerable Ursula was, of course, not foundress of the so-called Theatine nuns of Pescia, but of the Sisters of the Immaculate Conception of the Virgin Mary. Founded in Naples and placed under the spiritual direction of the Fathers of the Naples Oratory, the Sisters were put under the charge of the Theatine Order by Pope Urban VIII in 1633. Gaetano Moroni, *Dizionario di erudizione storico ecclesiastica*, vol. 73 (Venice, 1855), pp. 31–109.

57. On these functions of visionaries see Christian, *Apparitions in Spain*, pp. 184–87; Bynum, *Jesus as Mother*, pp. 181, 196; Weinstein and Bell, *Saints and Society*, pp. 153–54.

Chapter Five: The Second Investigation

1. "They [the Theatine nuns] have among themselves a mother superior [abbess] under whose rule they govern themselves, the Mistress of the Novices, and the other customary offices." ASPi, *Conventi Soppressi*, 924, ins. 1.

2. According to the report submitted to the provost, the men she named were worth over 10,000 scudi each. ASF, *Reggio Diritto*, fols. 1005, 1009.

3. The responsibilities of abbesses were outlined in numerous works of advice to nuns as well as in the written constitutions of many convents. For a sixteenth-century example, see St. Teresa, "Constitutions," in *The Complete Works*, 3: 219–38.

4. Accounts of these events are related in two reports, one entitled "Relatione della visita fatta alle Monache Theatine," and the other, "Abstratto del Processo di Benedetta." ASF, *Misc. Med.* 376, ins. 28, unnumbered pages.

5. "Abstratto," *ibid.*

6. The Council of Trent did not provide formally for triennial elections, but this became common practice during the reforms of the sixteenth and early seventeenth centuries. That the Theatine nuns of Pescia adhered to the practice can be seen from the entries recorded in the diary of Pio Ceci, a Pesciatine man whose daughter, later in the century, was elected to the post several times. Pescia, Biblioteca Comunale, I.B.52, fol. 74v.

7. The undated report sent to the nunzio bears the title *Breve discorso delle cose che si dicono della Madre Suor Benedetta Carlini da Vellano delle Teatine di Pescia*. The earliest probable date for its composition is that of Alfonso Giglioi's appointment as papal nuncio. The later date is that of the earliest probable date for a second report. See note 14. Another clue about the dating of the *Breve discorso* is the fact that Father Ricordati, who died in October, 1623, is mentioned in the present tense.

Although the *Breve discorso* does not state for whom it was written, the identity of the intended reader can be surmised from the sequence of events summarized in the *Abstratto del Processo di Benedetta*, in which the initials A. A. appear in the margin. These were the initials of the nuncio, Alfonso, Bishop of Anglona. the *Abstratto*, begins with the statement, "Having gone to Pescia under the orders given to us by your Illustrious and Most Reverend Lord at Siena, and after having considered the *processo*, which was made of the events that occurred in the person of Mother Benedetta Carlini of Vellano . . . , the previous *discorso*, considered by your Illustrious and Most Reverend Lord, was written . . ." ASF, *Misc. Med.* 376, ins. 28.

8. This conclusion and the others that follow come from the *Breve discorso*, ASF, *Misc. Med.*, 376, ins. 28. Changing conceptions of sanctity are discussed in Bell and Weinstein, *Saints and Society*, pp. 141–63. The Church's efforts to limit the influence of popular veneration and to extend the papacy's own power over canonization were boosted with the creation of the Congregation of Rites in the late sixteenth century and the publication of standardized procedures for canonization by Urban VIII in the early seventeenth century. See Edward W. Kemp, *Canonization and Authority in the Western Church* (Oxford, 1948).

9. Names had great significance both because they allowed one to discover whether angels were demonic or divine and because they had magic properties. Excorcist's manuals, such as those written in the late sixteenth century by Girolamo Menghi, often recommend that the procedure start by asking the presumed devil to reveal his name. D. P. Walker, *Unclean Spirits: Possession and Exorcism in France and England in the Late Sixteenth and Early Seventeenth Centuries* (Philadelphia, 1981), pp. 24–25.

10. The relationship between female mystics and their father confessors were complex and difficult. Often a reversal of roles took place, and the mystic went from being a spiritual daughter to being a spiritual guide. In the case of St. Catherine of Siena, for example, the confessor became a "son" to Catherine, whom he now called "mother." The problem with this inversion is that it made it more difficult for the confessor to mediate between the mystic and the clerical hierarchy, whose approval the mystic needed in order to be perceived as a saint. For a subtle analysis of the confessor's role, see Ciammitti, "Una santa di meno," pp. 603–39.

11. The charge of demonic obsession or posession became increasingly frequent in late sixteenth- and early seventeenth-century France and Italy. The most famous such case, popularized in the twentieth century by Aldous Huxley, involved the nuns at the Ursuline convent of Loudon; Huxley, *The Devils of Loudon* (London,

1952). A more sophisticated treatment of the same event can be found in Michel de Certeau, *La Possession de Loudon* (Paris, 1980). In Italy, where charges of witchcraft were rare, clear and careful distinctions were made between it and demonic possession or obsession. A witch was much more actively involved in the commission of sinful acts than was someone who was possessed. Witches also displayed different physical symptoms so that ecclesiastical officials and physicians could differentiate the two types. Similarly, possession entailed the devil's more vigorous control of his victim than did mere obsession. On the differences among these states and the consequences they had for the treatment of the accused, see among others, D. P. Walker, *Unclean Spirits*, pp. 10–17; E. William Monter, "French and Italian Witchcraft," *History Today*, 30 (Nov. 1980): 31–35; Giuseppe Bonomo, *Caccia alle streghe: La credenza nelle streghe dal sec. XIII al XIX con particolare riferimento all'Italia* (Palermo, 1971); T. K. Oesterreich, *Possession: Demoniacal and Other* (London, 1930), pp. 77–80.

12. Fear of mountain people's associations with the devil is noted also in F. Braudel, *The Mediterranean*, 1:34–38; and Hugh Trevor-Roper, "The European Witch-craze of the Sixteenth and Seventeenth Centuries," in *Religion, the Reformation, and Social Change* (London, 1967), pp. 104–8.

13. As a literary theme, the violence, ignorance, and gullibility of mountain people developed as a variant on the more general *satira del villano*. Dante called them "sour swine, indecent beasts more fit to grub and grunt for acorns than to sit to bread and wine." Giovanni Sercambi, Sacchetti, and Poggio Bracciolini, among others, had similar views. Renaissance attitudes are discussed in Giovanni Cherubini, "La società dell'appennino settentrionale (secoli XIII-XV)," in his *Signori, contadini, borghesi: Ricerche sulla società italiana del basso medioevo* (Florence, 1974), pp. 121–42. The hereditary component in accusations of witchcraft and diabolism was often used to strengthen the case against the accused. See Norman Cohn, *Europe's Inner Demons* (New York, 1975), p. 249; and Midelfort, *Witch Hunting*, pp. 186–87.

14. ASF, *Misc. Med.*, 376, ins. 28 contains two copies of this report. One is untitled and the other is called "Abstratto del Processo di Benedetta." Although undated, the report was probably written before November 1623, when a "Final Report" was written,

but after March 1623. This last date is founded on a reference in the report to Benedetta's death and resurrection, which allegedly occurred "two years before on the day of the Annunciation to the Virgin." Since that event occurred on the day of the Annunciation (March 25) after the death of Benedetta's father, and he was still alive in November 1620, the earliest date for the report would have to be March 25, 1623.

15. This conclusion as well as the ones that follow are all contained in the "Abstratto del Processo."

16. Several nuns testified that she sometimes laughed and made fun of her own partisans within the convent.

17. An account of the Fathers of the Holy Annunciation and their merger with the Barnabites can be found in Manzini, *L'apostolato di Pescia*.

18. The importance of these factors has been emphasized by Jean Sallmann's study of four late-sixteenth century Neapolitan women who claimed to be mystics. The authorities judged three of them to be frauds. The fourth, Ursula Benincasa, after some initial skepticism by the papacy, was accepted as a genuine visionary and eventually became a saint. What differentiated Ursula from the other three women were her social ties to the aristocracy, her relationship to a powerful confessor, and the institutional protection derived from her affiliation with a large religious order. Jean-Michael Sallmann, "La saintetè mystique feminine a Naples," in Sofia Boesch Gajano and Lucia Sebastiani, eds., *Culto dei Santi: Istituzioni e classi sociali in età preindustriale* (Rome, 1984), pp. 681–702.

19. A few cases of sexual relationships had turned up in the house for repentant prostitutes in Milan (*convertite*), but it is doubtful that these had become known to many people. On the function and organization of houses for repentant prostitutes, see Ruth Prelowski Liebowitz, "Conversion or Confinement? Houses for Repentant Prostitutes in Late Renaissance Italy," Paper presented at the Sixteenth Century Studies Conference (St. Louis, 1980); also the work of Sherrill Cohen on the *convertite* of Florence, forthcoming as a Ph.D. diss., Princeton, 1985.

20. This description comes from the private diary of a Theatine nun. ASPi, *Conventi Soppressi* 924, ins. 1.

21. Testimony of 1 August, 1619.

22. Elissa Weaver, "Spiritual Fun: A Study of Sixteenth-Century Tuscan Convent Theater," in M. B. Rose, ed., *Changing Perspectives on Medieval and Renaissance Women* (Syracuse, 1985). In some instances, the nuns would play male parts in tableaux that recreated the life of the holy family. St. Catherine Ricci, for example, took part in such a reenactment at her convent in Prato. See S. Razzi, *Suor Caterina de' Ricci.*

23. In his analysis of possession in ecstatic religions, the anthropologist I. M. Lewis persuasively argues that for many people and cultures, spirit possession is real, a cultural phenomenon whose validity and credibility should not be questioned by the scholar unless the actors themselves express doubts about them. To this extent, possession is an apt term to describe cases like Benedetta's, and one that locates her condition within the cultural matrix of her own society. But this does not preclude scholars from asking questions about the motivations of the people they are studying or placing their analysis within social, anthropological, or psychological frameworks that can only enrich their understanding of a set of events. The interpretation presented here is consistent both with modern anthropological and psychiatric observations or with those of premodern times. Each of these points of view adds unique elements to our perceptions regardless of the label attached to Benedetta's condition.

From an anthropological perspective, it is important to note that the disappearance of Benedetta's ailments after she received the stigmata and began to speak with the voice of other-worldly creatures—Splenditello and Jesus—fits a commonly observed pattern in the emergence of shamans in a variety of cultures. From being the passive victim of spirits that assail him (though far from passive with regard to other mortals), the would-be intercessor with the divine begins to master the spirits and becomes their partner. Illness gives way to the ability to do extraordinary deeds and thus to transcend nature. From this comes, for example, the ability to heal others or to prevent them from becoming ill. In the case of Benedetta, her new relationship with the realm of the divine allowed her to shield Pesciatines from plague and shortened their time in Purgatory. Often the change from subservience to partnership is expressed in the image of a marriage. Not surprisingly, Benedetta's mystical marriage with Jesus occurred shortly after she began to speak with his voice and that of his angel. Lewis, *Ecstatic Religion*, pp. 187–90.

This progression from illness to the assumption of other voices and personalities has also been observed by psychiatrists studying multiple personality disorder. It might be argued that for Benedetta, conversion-like symptoms were the prelude to a severe dissociative reaction, as her ability to resolve her problems gradually became less effective. Unable to come to terms with her conflicting desires, and ridden by guilt and a strong sense of sin about her sexual behavior, Benedetta may have detached what was unacceptable to her by creating a separate personality. Splenditello may have allowed her to fulfill some of her wishes without rejecting the values and desires of Benedetta. The mechanism that enabled her to do this was partial memory loss.

In common with modern day people who have multiple personality disorder, Benedetta exhibited a number of other traits. She was impressionable and easily influenced (e.g., when her confessor told her to suffer, she did; when he allowed her to have a vision, she did). Her dominant, public personality was a model of good behavior (she was humble and obedient). And she forgot many of the events concerning her other selves (she could not recall having written to the provost or talking about how to decorate the chapel for her wedding). On dissociative reactions and multiple personalities, see Ernest R. Hilgard, *Divided Consciousness: Multiple Controls in Human Thought and Action* (New York, 1977); *Diagnostic and Statistical Manual of Mental Disorders*, American Psychiatric Association, 3rd. ed. (Washington, D.C., 1980).

The psychiatric interpretation does not, of course, imply that mystics like Benedetta were mad, dysfunctional, or marginal figures in their cultures. Although a few contemporaries, such as the sixteenth-century physician Johann Weyer, and even larger numbers of modern scholars have attributed claims of possession (and witchcraft) to madness, the relationship is tenuous. In this regard it is important to remember that while insanity might have been seen by the authorities as the cause of Benedetta's condition, they focused instead on demonic possession and deception. Madness and possession could be related—melancholia made it easier for the devil to assail his victim—but in Benedetta's case, as in most other cases of possession, the link was not made. Opinions about

madness and demonic possession by contemporaries such as Johann Schenk, Johann Weyer, and Tommaso Garzoni are discussed
in M. Laignel-Lavastine and Jean Vinchon, *Les Malades de l'esprit et
leurs médecins du XVIe au XIXe siècle* (Paris, 1930). Catholic thought
on the causes, manifestation, and treatment of possession was
codified by Paul V's *Rituale Romunum* (1614). See also the aptly
skeptical views on the use and misuse of psychology in history by
H. E. Erik Midelfort, "Madness and the Problems of Psychological
History in the Sixteenth Century," *Sixteenth Century Journal*, 12:1
(1981):5–12.

24. The disappearance of Splenditello and the other supernatural
creatures that spoke through Benedetta can be explained either in
religious or psychological terms. Neither explanation implies deliberate fraud. It can be argued that multiple personalities appear
at first in order to protect a person in a situation of conflict that
threatens to overwhelm them. These additional personalities per-
form a positive function and are aware of the main personality and
its social and cultural predicament. Frequently, when they are no
longer needed, they quickly disappear.

25. "If anyone says that man's free will moved and aroused by
God, by assenting to God's call and action, in no way cooperates
toward disposing and preparing itself to obtain the grace of justification, that it cannot refuse its assent if it wishes, but that, as
something inanimate, it does nothing whatever and is merely passive, let him be anathema." *Council of Trent*, sixth session, fourth
canon, pp. 42–43.

Epilogue

1. ASPi, *Corp. Relig.*, 924, ins. 1.

2. The report, addressed to "Your Serene Highnesses" (*Seren-
issime Altezze*), is a brief four-point summary of the report to the
nunzio. After a statement of certainty regarding Benedetta's deception at the hands of the devil, it outlines the investigators'
findings about the miraculous signs as well as the heterosexual
and lesbian accusations against Benedetta. ASPi, *Misc. Med.* 376,
ins. 28.

3. Crompton, "Lesbian Impunity," p. 17; Henri Estienne, *Apol-*

ogie pour Herodote; Michel Montaigne, *Diary of a Journey to Italy in 1580 and 1581* in *The Complete Works* (Stanford, 1948), pp. 869–70; E. W. Monter, "La Sodomie."

4. A series of Venetian laws reveal the concern with dress as an expression of gender relations. In the late fifteenth and sixteenth centuries, some of the fashions in women's clothing and hairstyle seemed to the authorities to blur gender lines. These fashions were prohibited by patriarchal order, under penalty of excommunication, because they were "a kind of sodomy." Particularly prone to dressing in a masculine way were the numerous prostitutes of the city, who adopted manly attire in an effort to compete for male clients with male homosexuals. Patricia Labalme, "Sodomy and Venetian Justice in the Renaissance," *Tijdschrift voor Rechtsgeschiedens* (*The Legal History Review*), 52:3 (1984):247–51.

5. It is, of course, difficult to make firm generalizations based on a small number of cases. In seventeenth-century Leiden, for instance, the only two cases of lesbian sexuality that have come to light involved transvestism, but the accused women were flogged and banished rather than executed; Dirk Jaap Noordam, "Homosocial relations in Leiden (1533–1811)," in *Among Men, Among Women: Sociological and Historical Recognition of Homosocial Arrangements* (Amsterdam, 1983), pp. 218–23. On the other hand, the two executions that took place in France both involved transvestism, and in each only the "male" in the relationship was killed. Similarly, in Germany execution was recommended only for the transvestite partner in a sexual relationship between two early eighteenth-century women; Brigitte Eriksson, "A Lesbian Execution in Germany, 1721: The Trial Records," *Journal of Homosexuality*, 6:1/2 (Fall/Winter 1980/81): 27–40. In Spain, according to Gomez, only those who used material instruments were executed; the others were whipped and sent to the galleys.

The need to resolve issues of gender unambiguously severely tested the authorities when they occasionally confronted cases of hermaphroditism. Here it was not a question of an individual representing himself as something he was not, but of being both male and female in sex. Physicians and jurists usually agreed that the individual determine once and for all which gender to adopt. After this decision was made, it was a capital offense to adopt the dress or behavior of the other sex. See Stephen Greenblatt, "Loudon and London," *Critical Inquiry*, 12 (in press).

Two episodes that reveal perhaps more clearly than others the importance of transvestism both for the authorities and the accused are the trial of Joan of Arc and the less well-known trial of a young girl in southern France in the late sixteenth century. The most serious charge against St. Joan was not her lack of sexual purity, which she had demonstrated beyond a shadow of a doubt, but her dressing in male garments. Although she might well point out that in the early days of the church several female saints had also passed themselves off as men, the context for such actions had changed and so had the tolerance of the authorities. Indeed, the very hierarchy of values, which associated virtue, courage, and the pursuit of holiness with the male sex and which held that a woman became a man when she served Christ, made it inevitable both that women would transgress dress codes and other gender rules and that society would punish them harshly for doing so. Marina Warner, *Joan of Arc: The Image of Female Heroism* (New York, 1980); Vern L. Bullough, "Transvestism in the Middle Ages," in V. Bullough and J. Brundage, *Sexual Practices and the Medieval Church*, pp. 43–54; John Anson, "Female Monks: The Transvestite Motif in Early Christian Literature," *Viator*, 5 (1974):1–32.

As for the young girl who was accused of transvestism in southern France almost two centuries later, unlike St. Joan, she was not sexually pure, but she showed the same kind of courage, and her behavior raised similar fears about women who usurped male prerogatives. After abandoning her home town, Marie, as she was known, discarded her female dress, became a weaver, and took on a wife. According to Montaigne, who had heard of the case while traveling in the area, when the authorities discovered her true sex, she was brought to trial and sentenced to be hanged, "which she said she would rather endure than to return to the state of a girl." Implicit in Marie's statement is the likelihood that she was offered a lighter sentence if she agreed to return to her proper station in life. As suggested both by her statement and by the fact that her "wife" did not share her fate, the authorities' real concern was not her sexual crime but her violation of gender relations. Her refusal to conform and the authorities' response is a telling commentary on the constraints faced by women in early modern France. Montaigne, *Journey to Italy*, pp. 869–70.

6. The two best known examples from the sixteenth century are Magdalena de la Cruz and Maria de la Visitación. Magdalena, who claimed to "see" the battle of Pavia, gained such influence that when the future king Philip II of Spain was born, he was wrapped in her robes for special protection. Eventually, both Magdalena and Maria were sentenced to solitary imprisonment within their convents.

7. St. Teresa, "Constitution," in *Complete Works*, vol. 3, pp. 236–37.

8. *Ibid*.

9. Measures such as these are recommended by St. Teresa as well as by other authorities. The sentences against Magdalena de la Cruz and Maria de la Visitación contain these provisions, as do the constitutions of several sixteenth and seventeenth century female orders.

Index